Flying with No. 20 Squadron, 1918

Flying with No. 20 Squadron, 1918

An RFC/RAF Observer Over the Western
Front During the First World War

ILLUSTRATED

With a Bristol Fighter Squadron
Walter Noble

Aeroplane Design
By F. S. Barnwell

LEONAUR

Flying with No. 20 Squadron, 1918
An RFC/RAF Observer Over the Western Front During the First World War
With a Bristol Fighter Squadron
by Walter Noble
and
Aeroplane Design
By F. S. Barnwell

ILLUSTRATED

FIRST EDITION IN THIS FORM

First published under the titles
With a Bristol Fighter Squadron
and
Aeroplane Design and A Simple Explanation of Inherent Stability

Leonaur is an imprint of Oakpast Ltd
Copyright in this form © 2025 Oakpast Ltd

ISBN: 978-1-917666-14-5 (hardcover)
ISBN: 978-1-917666-15-2 (softcover)

http://www.leonaur.com

Publisher's Notes

The views expressed in this book are not necessarily
those of the publisher.

Contents

Yours truly
W. Noble.

With a Bristol Fighter Squadron

Contents

Contents

To
My Father and Mother

Introduction

By Winston S. Churchill

War Office,
Whitehall,
S.W.1.
27th October, 1919.

The author of this book has a good fighting record and is entitled to write with authority upon the episodes which have come within his own experience. I am told by those who are qualified to judge that the lessons which may be derived from this straightforward and soldierly narrative possess a definite value among the records of the Royal Air Force in the Great War.

The story is certainly of vivid interest to those who wish to form a lively and a true impression of the kind of things our young officers did in the immortal period which has just closed. Nothing that has ever happened in the world before has offered to man such an opportunity for individual personal prowess as the air fighting of the Great War. Fiction, has never portrayed such extraordinary combats, such hairbreadth escapes, such absolute superiority to risk, such dazzling personal triumphs. The devotion and courage of the airman was no higher than that of his comrade on the land or on the sea; nor were his trials or sufferings greater. But the battle to the death in the high air called forth a combination, for the purposes of war, of spirit, eye and hand more complete and more harmonious than any previously believed to be within the range of human nature.

It is in this light that these pages deserve to be read.

Winston S. Churchill

CHAPTER 1

A Fight with Triplanes

Squadron orders posted in flight messes one dull foggy evening in late January, 1918, read as follows:—

"O.P: (Offensive Patrol). *Pow-wow* 8.0. Lines 9.0-10.30."

Then followed the names of nine pilots and observers detailed for the "show," whose role was to remain one-and-a-half hours to the east of the German lines and seek out and destroy hostile machines.

For some days a low-lying ground-mist had prevented us from indulging in this exhilarating, if somewhat nerve-racking pastime. However, the morning turned out clear and sunny, with a slight westerly breeze. Having donned our flying kit, the hour appointed for the *pow-wow* found us congregated outside the office into which the sepulchral haunting notes of a Klaxon horn bade us enter. Here the major awaited us. Familiarly known as the "Old Man" by the more youthful members of his command, this hardy veteran of some thirty-two summers was, and still is, one of the most popular squadron commanders on the Western Front.

He proceeded to call the roll:—

"Knapp." "Here, sir." 'Breamer." "Here, sir." "Two streamers on your tail." "Badham and Wells on the right of K." "Sims and Lovat on the left of K."

The formation of nine machines was subdivided into groups of three, of which these comprised the first, Badham and Sims flying slightly higher than Knapp, the formation leader, and to his right and left rear respectively.

"Jackson and Creasy, streamer on your right strut."

"Doone and Sturgess on the right of Jackson."

"Long and Yardell on the left of Jackson."

"Young and Trott, streamer on your left strut."

15

"Farman and Erleigh on the right of Young."

"Dallas and Mooney on the left of Young."

"Jackson's formation on the right of Knapp's."

"Young's formation on the left of Knapp's."

Jackson and Young were sub-leaders, and in correct formation flying their groups would be equidistant from the leader and as far above him and to his right and left rear respectively as had, from experience, been found necessary.

Having read out the order in which to leave the ground, the C.O. dismissed us with the final exhortation, "See if you can't get some more Huns today." We repaired to the aerodrome, where our machines—seemingly as impetuous and eager to be off as our newest pilot fresh from England—awaited us.

After a hasty but thorough inspection of the flying apparatus—that crazy structure of wood and fabric plus engine upon which so much depends—we climbed into our seats where, sitting back to back, we looked round our respective cockpits to see that everything was in order. Pilots looked to their instruments, whilst observers, who had previously fired a few rounds through their Lewis Gun, swung round the mounting on which it revolves to see that it worked freely, examined the ammunition drums, arranged spare gun parts so that in the event of a regrettable jam as little time as possible might be lost in remedying it, and made sure that maps and other necessaries were ready for use.

On a wave of the hand from the C.O., the leader took off, followed at intervals, of a few seconds by the rest of the formation. In threes we circled round the aerodrome, steadily gaining height. When at about 4,500 feet from the ground a red light fired by the flight commander's observer warned us to get into formation, as we were about to make for the lines.

Sub-leaders who had, until now, been acting independently, at once led their groups to their appointed positions; and still climbing we flew due east towards the battlefield of the skies—a terrain bounded on the west by the enemy's trenches and to the east by the ever-increasing audacity and confidence of flight commanders.

In a few minutes we were looking down—upon Ypres—immortal in the annals of Belgium, of England, of Canada, of the Empire.

In the far-distant days before: Hell-Let-Loose made its headquarters in Europe it was, as Conan Doyle has so aptly written, "*A relic of the soul of other days, a poet's dream, a wanderer's romance.*" Now it lies in the dust. Day by day, year by year, its architectural splendours crumble and decay. Yet the spirit, the soul, the intangible, incomprehensible influence of the venerable city casts its spell on all who tramp her desolate by-ways, who gaze from the skies upon her beauty, complacent even in death.

The day was a perfect one. Above, "the inverted bowl we call the sky," free from clouds and beautified by the wintry sun. The suspicion of a breeze speeded our progress slightly on the outward flight, but promised no formidable opposition to our return. To the south the Lys reflected its waters in shimmering, golden radiance; whilst far away massive, triangular Lille lay awaiting deliverance. To the north the flooded area swollen by the recent thaw rested in tranquil repose connecting the Yser Canal with the sea. In the distance the cliffs of Dover and the outline of the English coast—alluring and inviting— served to mingle thoughts of the nightmare of the present with visions of the past and dreams of the future.

The machine in which I was flying as observer was on the leader's right with the bulk of the formation straggling somewhat behind and above us at altitudes ranging from 13,000 to 16,000 feet. On reaching Zillebeke Lake, we all turned north and crossed the lines at their intersection of the Forêt d'Houthulst which spread itself out, naked and desolate, in grotesque outlines below us, its leafless and shattered branches stretching out imploring hands to an unsympathetic and pre-occupied world.

Dim and dark as the Stygian Groves, it harboured a swarm of the airman's *bêtes noires*—Archibald, the anti-aircraft gun, known to us endearingly and platonically as Archie. At the commencement of the current year the Forest Gunners shared with those of Wervicq the honour of having gained our respect and admiration far in advance of their kin in other districts. Later, Steenwercke, for a time, held pride of place.

Today, as usual, the shooting was wonderfully good. A few sighting shots burst far ahead; but on warming to their work, dark black masses of smoke arrived, apparently from nowhere, until each machine was surrounded by its own particular satellites. Yet so difficult is it for a landsman, even with the latest devices of science at his command, to hit a small object, scarcely discernible, two-and-a-half or more miles away moving at a speed at least equal to that of an express train that, on this occasion, the entire formation passed unscathed through a very heavy and well directed barrage.

When a novice to the gentle art of Hun strafing, one attaches little importance to the usually vain efforts of the anti-aircraft guns. Their bark is infinitely worse than their bite—except, of course, on the (fortunately) very rare occasions when a direct hit scatters machine and occupants to the four winds of heaven.

Personally, during over 200 hours of flying over Hunland, I have not witnessed the total wreckage of an aeroplane, nor have I seen one brought down out of control by fire from land batteries. It is, however, by no means an uncommon occurrence for machines to be compelled to return to their aerodrome, or to make a forced landing in unknown country (with its attendant dangers) owing to disabilities caused to personnel, machine or engine by flying metal. On two occasions my pilot and I have had to leave the formation with our engine in a parlous state—of which more *anon*.

Being at this period of my aerial adventure in the novitiate stage, I amused myself vastly by firing a few rounds at all bursts within close range. A percentage of bullets used in the air have an incendiary composition pressed in at the base. This burning fiercely, one is enabled to trace the course of one's rounds. They are known as "tracers." It is fascinating to watch them entering and passing through the black seething masses; also, it is excellent practice in marksmanship, and for that reason can be recommended to young and enthusiastic observers.

Furthermore, it gives one some slight occupation in addition to searching the skies for hostile aircraft. When, after some months of war-flying one's nerves become jaded and worn, any diversion that takes one's thoughts from grim and tragic possibilities is not to be despised. To think of danger, to allow one's imagination to run riot—either when flying or during the intervals thereof—is to hold out endearing arms to the Goddess of Nerves who sooner or later inevitably installs herself as the mistress of all flying men.

Leaving the forest and a pathway of black trailing smudges behind us, we were soon to the east of Dixmude—the scene of much strenuous endeavour in the early days of the war, and now rivalling Ypres in picturesque desolation. Nieuport and Ostend were clearly visible, their waterways blinking in the sun, whilst far away to the right lay Bruges, of belfry fame. Still further removed, the islands in the mouth of the Scheldt revealed themselves, in hazy and indistinct outlines.

Now following the leader, we turned; and presently were skirting the eastern fringe of the forest. Suddenly I perceived a trail of whitish smoke vanishing earthwards in the rear of the flight commander's machine. I pointed this out to my pilot, and placed a finger on the red circle of paint above his head. Not having seen the descending ball of flame, but only the smoke from it, I came incorrectly to the conclusion that a red light had been fired. This is the signal employed by the leader to inform his followers that he is about to attack.

It may also be used by him to rally the formation when through devices of the enemy or from other causes it has become split up. When fired by another member of the flight it is a call for assistance. White and green lights are also carried. The former is fired from the leader's machine when, owing perhaps to inclement weather, he determines to abandon the expedition. The latter is used by any member of the formation when engine or other trouble makes a return to the aerodrome imperative.

In this case the leader's engine was not working smoothly, and his observer fired a green light from his Very pistol. Imagining it to be a red one, we searched north, south, east and west, in the sun, in the heavens, and in the depths below for hostile aircraft. No Hunnish silhouettes revealed themselves.

Sailing along complacently again, it suddenly dawned upon us that we had made a mistake. Far away in the distance, rapidly fading out of sight, were the bulk of the formation, whilst the leader was left with our machine and one other. As we crossed the lines a second green light explained the mystery. The first had, of course, been observed by the remainder of the formation; upon which, the second leader had taken charge, and all machines should have followed him.

The "lame duck" being immune from molestation on our side of the lines, we accompanied our companion on a tour of the trenches until, being joined by another, we flew east for a couple of miles and then turned north.

Shortly afterwards three strange craft passed by—600 or more yards away—going in the opposite direction. They were German Triplanes, and it was the first appearance of this type on our part of the front for many months. We came to the conclusion that it was the navy out for an airing, and continued our peaceful course unsuspiciously.

Events occur suddenly—with dramatic, swiftness—in the air. At one moment the occupants of a fighting plane are at peace with the world, congratulating themselves on immunity from attack, or itching for a fight, according to their individual temperaments. The next, they are fighting to kill or be killed—every sense on the alert—all they possess of brain, muscle, nerve and resource concentrated on the fleeting opportunity.

Perceiving that we had been deceived and were off our guard, the Hun pilots had given no sign of hostile intent, but had stealthily gained height, thereby winning the tactical advantage, whilst at the same time proving themselves to be old hands at the game by inclining eastwards, thereby placing themselves between us and the sun.

It is essential to treat all machines as hostile when in doubt. An experienced observer in the machine on our right had kept an eye on the strangers. On their turning and diving on us he at once fired a red light and thereby saved us from the possibly fatal result of our feeling of false security.

The scrap resolved itself into three duels, each Hun having selected his adversary. The fights in which the other two machines were engaged were indecisive. In both cases the enemy eventually broke off the combat and turned back, after having found themselves too adjacent to our lines for their peace of mind.

In the meantime, the Tripe that had singled out our machine for destruction was diving on us and was now within about 350 yards. Awakening to the situation I tapped my pilot on the head and pointed out the rapidly approaching Hun. He acted at once—turned, so as to face the enemy machine, and put his nose down slightly, thus putting the opposing pilot off his aim and causing him to sweep over and past us. Then as we zoomed up, I was enabled to get a magazine off at the still diving Hun. My aim was directed at the pilot's seat, and although tracers appeared to enter both cockpit and engine, no serious damage could have been inflicted, for he showed no signs of wishing to retire from the combat.

We had how the inestimable advantage of height. As we turned to dive, the Hun sat on his tail and fired a burst at us. The range was too great for accurate shooting, however, for not even a wing was perforated. When we had closed to within 150 yards, the German pilot put his machine into a spin. We followed him down, my pilot firing a long burst at him. Before he had come out of the spin, and thus provided an easier target, my pilot ceased firing and zoomed up. Unfortunately, his gun had jammed. The Hun, doubtless thanking whatever gods there be for this respite, flattened out again some 200 yards below us.

We circled round him for a time whilst the jam was being remedied and I fired several short bursts whenever a favourable opportunity occurred. When once more ready for action, my pilot manoeuvred for position. Eventually he contrived to place himself in the Hun's rear so that he could dive on his tail. At the crucial moment he pushed forward the joy-stick and sent the machine hurtling through the air at terrific speed—roughly 200 miles per hour. The Hun pilot appeared to be surprised at this sudden renewal of the offensive by us. For some reason, known only to himself, he continued to fly straight. In an incredibly short period of time, we covered the intervening space.

Peering forward in the teeth of a wind pressure that made observation extremely difficult, I could distinctly see the back of the pilot's helmeted head and the colouring of the machine. The wings were painted a dirty, creamy white, whilst nose and body were encircled with red and black rings. National markings, the Maltese cross, were exceptionally small. When within about 80 yards, my pilot commenced to shoot. Following the line of fire, "tracers" were apparently entering the vital spots. Thirty rounds—fifty rounds—one hundred. Expectantly I awaited the denouement. At last, the Boche's painted nose inclined towards the earth. In a moment nose and tail were in one vertical line. Our machine flattened out, and, looking over the side, I watched the tiny black crosses on the lower plane growing smaller and still smaller as the fabric on which they were painted rushed headlong down through space.

In the air over Hunland one must allow nothing whatever—no matter how absorbing, interesting or important—to occupy one's whole attention. Always a lookout must be kept for hostile aircraft. Two Albatross Scouts, who had been hidden in the sun, now appeared slightly above us and some hundreds of yards to our rear. Our supply of ammunition being nearly exhausted, we were not in a position to act on the offensive. The lines were barely two miles away and we made for them. The Albatrii gained steadily upon us.

When they had crept up to within 300 yards, I fired a few short, well-aimed bursts, not so much with the idea of shooting one down as of warning them not to approach too near. The knowledge that the observer is awake and, on the alert, has usually a deterrent effect on German pilots. They would prefer, and naturally so—surprise being one of the most important factors of success in aerial warfare—to creep up unseen.

After firing nearly, a magazine of ammunition, my gun jammed and I found that the top extractor had broken. This can be remedied on the ground in a few seconds, but in the air, it takes somewhat longer. Every moment brought the Huns within more effective range, and already tracers were whizzing by, luckily wide of the mark. On informing my pilot of the difficulty, he opened the throttle to its fullest extent, and putting the nose of the machine down, raced for the lines. In as many seconds as it would have taken me to mend the gun, we were on our side of the line, and the Huns had beetled away eastwards.

On reaching the aerodrome we hurried to the office and put in a claim for a triplane out of control and hoped that confirmation would be forthcoming of its having crashed to earth. We rang up anti-aircraft batteries, balloon companies as well as the infantry and other squadrons, but without success. One is credited with the destruction of an enemy machine only when indisputable evidence of its having been destroyed is obtained.

We were, naturally, bitterly disappointed, as at the time we were quite sure that we had crashed the Hun. However, *"experientia docet"*—perhaps with greater rapidity in war flying than in any other pastime. We were then comparative beginners. We have since on many occasions seen enemy machines break off a fight and go down in a vertical nose dive or in a spin. When out of harm's way, they have flattened out as little damaged as the youthful British aviator who is destined to be disillusioned when his claim fails to obtain the—necessary verification.

This practice is employed much less by ourselves then by the enemy as a means of escape. When hopelessly outclassed or outnumbered, it provides an invaluable last card. Ball was once forced to use it; whilst Baron von Richthofen tells us that it was a favourite trick of his brother, Lothar, who on at least one occasion, after having employed it against one of our scouts that had the advantage of him in height, recovered his balance, got above his opponent and shot him down in flames. (*Vide Richthofen & Böelcke in Their Own Words* by Manfred Freiherr von Richthofen & Oswald Böelcke—*The Red Battle Flyer* by Manfred Freiherr von Richthofen & *An Aviator's Field Book* by Oswald Böelcke: Leonaur 2011.)

Now that most aerial fights take place over the German side of the trenches it may be readily realised that the enemy have every opportunity of putting into play this trick—if so, it may be termed. His pilots can dive or spin down to within 100 feet of the ground, and then flatten out, knowing perfectly well, that we cannot follow them down. On the other hand, our machines practising it are placed at a disadvantage.

The lower they descend the more difficult it becomes for them to make their way home in safety. A machine thus isolating itself becomes a prey for all German pilots in the sky who, having the advantage in height, should have little difficulty in destroying it, especially if it is some miles over Hunland. In addition, Archie singles it out for attention; and if, perchance, it has to descend very low, the infantry and machine-gunners have an innings.

CHAPTER 2

On Spinning Down

We were detailed for the afternoon "show," which was to look for trouble over the German lines from 2 till 3.30. Strangely enough, we were destined to receive further education in the utility of a spin as a means of escaping from a tight corner.

The sun had commenced its downward curve. In other respects, the stage setting closely resembled that of the morning We were flying at 16,000 to 18,000 feet, and the skies being clear of enemy aircraft we had pushed on towards the coast until Ostend sparkled, outwardly calm and peaceful, a few miles to the north. We had turned and were approaching Ghistelles when I noticed three machines half a mile or more behind us. I at once jumped to the conclusion that they were Huns and drew the attention of my pilot to them.

If there is one single accomplishment a fighting airman should possess—in addition to being a good shot—it is the ability to distinguish friends from foes. After a time one can do this instinctively. An experienced airman appears to sense a hostile machine when all that is visible is a black speck which the untrained eye would not even discern.

A plane approaching from the west is almost invariably piloted. by a British or Allied aviator. Not so those that come from Hunland. They must be watched until their outlines proclaim their nationality. Theoretically this knowledge of types of aircraft by silhouette appears very easy to acquire. In practice, it is only gained after constant experience, and there have been cases of promising pilots turning out lamentable failures through inability to complete their education in this respect.

The Belgians fly a type which bears some resemblance to a German machine, whilst the French have another. Nor is it the easiest thing in the world to be sure of the nationality of even our own

24

scouts when, out of pure devilry, they amuse themselves by diving on one's tail *pour passer le temps* in the absence of more legitimate prey. It is sound policy to credit with hostile intent all craft that fail by their silhouettes, markings or actings to give evidence of their amicability. It follows that a burst of fire has not infrequently served to remind a playful pilot that the other man is inexperienced, is taking no risks— or, as is often the case, is not entirely immune from flying nerves.

These three machines appeared to be flying in formation side by side as if bosom friends. As a matter of fact, the middle machine was one of ours that had failed to keep with us on the turn. While watching them, and musing as to what tactics the flight commander would employ to increase our already considerable bag of Huns, suddenly and without preliminaries a transformation scene took place. Instead of flying tranquilly and evenly in our wake, two machines were diving almost vertically on their late companion, which was spinning away from them. My first thought was that the Huns were stunting for our benefit. Not for some moments did I realise that a scrap was in progress. Hurriedly I counted up the machines in our immediate vicinity. Sure enough, one was missing, only eight remained. The ninth must be the one spinning down.

As I tapped my pilot on the head he, following others, swung round and we raced back. In the meantime, the occupants: of the strafed machine were experiencing exciting moments—and incidentally, were being reminded of the advisability of keeping in formation and not straggling. In passing, it is interesting to note that the pilot, a first-class airman, but with a modicum of experience in war-flying, developed later a tendency to leave the flight in search of the "odd" Hun, as a result of which—as was inevitable—he eventually "bought it," and was, together with his observer, taken prisoner.

On this occasion the latter had, apparently, been daydreaming; for it was not until there was an Albatross Scout 20 to 30 yards away on either side that he drew attention to the startling and mildly humorous incident. Where the Huns appeared from has never transpired, and why they did not shoot will always remain a mystery.

Possibly they mistook us for a formation of their own machines—a not altogether uncommon occurrence.

Our man wasted not a moment in throwing his machine into a spin. The Huns, galvanised into sudden activity, dived after him, firing sedulously the while. The target was by no means an easy one and whilst wings and fuselage were riddled with bullets, occupants and engine—in fact all vital parts—were untouched. Relief was now close at hand. Before we could be of any assistance, however, the spinning machine was flattened out, and the observer fired a magazine at one of his pursuers as he dived past him and sent him down completely out of control.

There remained a single Hun scout upon whom eight British two-seaters were converging. The formation leader arrived first within range. He fired about 100 rounds, after which he made a right-hand climbing turn which enabled his observer to carry on with the good work. The Albatross went down in a vertical nose dive some hundreds of feet—then the dive developed into a spin, and, revolving rhythmically on its axis, she was seen by us all to crash into a wood.

This was the first crash I had witnessed in aerial combat. To say that any feeling of pity for the luckless occupant possessed me would be to tell an unmitigated falsehood. To him I gave no thought. I was simply terrifically delighted in watching the downward course of the plane and fearful lest it should flatten out and cheat us after all; which was followed by a feeling of quiet satisfaction when it disappeared in the dim recesses of the wood.

It was not until our patrol was over, and we were heading for home, that it occurred to me that a man—a brother airman and, in all probability, a good sportsman—had gone to that Valhalla, midway between earth and heaven, to which are wafted the souls of all good flying men and boys. Even then, so little had I actually seen of the helmeted and goggled pilot, that it was hard to associate him with the beautiful, many-coloured, birdlike structure that the chances of war had decreed we should destroy.

A vivid mind can picture in imagination the sensations and thoughts of a doomed man falling headlong at tremendous speed through miles of space. It visualises the strained, drawn, agonised face of the pilot, his every sense impregnated with the fear of swift implacable fate. In front he sees, as in a grotesque dream, his now obsolete instruments and Death—around him, flimsy matchwood and canvas, against which presses and swirls the up-rushing air.

Yet we know from the lips of those who, by favour of the gods, have survived this unparalleled ordeal, that it is not so terrible after all. Personally, I have come down out of control from 14,000 to 6,000 feet. My experiences on this occasion are reserved for a subsequent chapter. I may say at once, however, that I was not unduly disturbed.

Vaguely it occurred to me that my adventures in many lands and in varied climes had, after many vicissitudes, come to an abrupt termination. I was curious as to how many moments would elapse before we reached *terra firma*, and what the end would be like. A feeling of utter detachment came over me as if one soul side of me were witnessing the final scene of the last act in my life drama. Acute, all-absorbing fear was absent.

So, I believe it is in the majority of cases when machines continue out of control until the mad rush is checked by contact with Mother Earth.

But how can this be explained? Why should it be so? A drowning man is said to view his past life in kaleidoscopic detail. Before passing to another world he sees in a comprehensive, all-embracing flash the ill deeds and mayhap—if the gods are merciful—some of the chivalrous acts of his career.

It is my experience that the higher we ascend into the purer, lighter air of the upper regions, the more cheerful, optimistic and imbued with the joy of life we become. It is known that airmen sing for very joy and lightness of heart when far up in the azure blue. The words may be the latest brainwave of the mess entertainer; but the spirit behind them changes the crudest effort into a song of happiness—a song of exultation over all that can hurt—a song of mastery over everything that can kill.

Airmen, will, I think, agree with me when I say that the very stoutest of our number passes through moments during which he has what is described in Airmanese as "colossal wind-up" before setting off on a show, with its limitless prospects of danger; and that a feeling of serenity and gladness takes its place as he climbs heavenwards. Nerves become steady once again and he longs for a scrap to relieve the boredom of flying molested only by Archie. He becomes supremely indifferent to everything that has power to inflict injury upon him.

In brief, it is my considered opinion that being brought down out of control is not the hideous nightmare that one would suppose.

At all events, I like to think I am right, and that the glorious company of youthful airmen—someone's sons who "have spilled out the sweet red wine of youth"—have passed in a flash to the other side calmly serene, having tasted nought of fear or of remorse or vain regrets in their dramatic transference. Perhaps the gods have been kind to them, in that in dying for their country—whether for our Island Empire or for Germany—they have in a bound attained to the highest pinnacle of fame and honour, whilst still youthful, still cherishing ideals, living yet in a land of dreams in which they weep for no illusions lost—no hope deferred. Beloved of the gods they have died young.

They shall not grow old
As we that are left grow old.
Age shall not weary them nor the years condemn.
At the going down of the sun and in the morning
We will remember them.

CHAPTER 3

First Kill Over the Salient

"Allied Air Successes" in large headlines cheered the British Public on opening their favourite morning paper one day in late January, 1918. Never since the outbreak of war had the operations of our airmen been carried out on such an extensive scale or in such a variety of ways.

I quote the Report on Fighting only, that being the branch in which we specialised:—

Hard air fighting took place yesterday all along the line, the results being greatly in our favour. Ten hostile aeroplanes were brought down and six others driven down out of control. One of our machines is missing.

★★★★★★★★★★

It is interesting to compare this report with the results achieved on a certain day in October, when in air fighting sixty-eight enemy aircraft were destroyed and twenty-six driven down out of control, with a loss to us of seventeen machines missing.

★★★★★★★★★★

This demonstrates unmistakably the giant strides made in the aerial services of both ourselves and the Germans. Whilst I will not now attempt to juggle with the Parliamentary phrase "Supremacy of the air," I can, from personal experience, assure the reader that our ascendancy had become more marked, week by week and month by month, throughout the year. It is of the part played by the squadron to which I had the honour and great good fortune to belong that I propose to write. Of the sixteen enemy aeroplanes shot down we were responsible for seven, whilst the "missing" machine was unfortunately one of our formation.

For some days the earth had been covered with a mantle of snow, and dense low-lying fogs had greatly hindered war flying. On the rare occasions when we had taken the air for a practice flight, we had been amply rewarded for the inconvenience entailed by the impressive, picturesque grandeur of a world clad in virginal white, from which scintillated glistening pinpoints of silver radiance.

Now, however, after a forty-eight hours' thaw, except for vestiges of snow where the rays of the sun had not penetrated, the countryside had reverted to its normal wintry state of mud and bleakness. Twelve machines were detailed to provide, in the absence of anything more thrilling, practice for the Boche anti-aircraft gunners from 11.0 to 12.30. Visibility was moderately good and at 10,000 feet we had an excellent bird's-eye view of the famous Ypres salient and of pockmarked area adjoining it.

Everywhere canals and rivers had overflowed, and to the north of Dixmude the flooded terrain had swollen visibly. The sinuous winding lines of opposing trenches could be followed without difficulty. In these comparatively peaceful days before the April withdrawal, we held a tiny portion of the vast Forest of Houthulst and the line passed to the east of Poelcappelle and Passchendaele, west of Gheluvelt through Hollebeke and east of Messines. Not even on the Somme battlefields can one see a more pitiful, desolate stretch of once fertile country.

These plains of Flanders are low-lying; and shell-holes, innumerable and interlaced, have penetrated below the water-level. That day the loathsomeness of the scene beggared description, and I was thankful that we were at an altitude which precluded detailed impressions of the ghastliness of the spectacle. Picture, if you can, gentle reader devoid of war experience: countless mammoth bodies in the most virulent stage of smallpox, encircle the hideous gaping sores with—by way of contrast—pure, blushing snow, and you have a slight idea of this abode of phantom shapes and decomposing matter.

I was reminded of Dante's choice of punishment for those who were "*sad in the sweet air*" of an abiding dwelling place 'neath the foul marsh. For miles east and west of the trenches extended this damning evidence of human nature at its worst. The huge Messines Craters, filled to the brim with khaki slime, stood out in all their lonely impressiveness—excrescences on the fair face of a demented world. Of erstwhile peaceful hamlets or of roads there was no trace discernible. It was a relief to look further afield and notice how shell holes became fewer and roads more apparent until presently shades of green and brown marked where fruitful production had taken the place of wanton destruction.

And Ypres—immortal, unconquerable its soul; dead, shapeless, mutilated its body—as day by day we have ploughed the heavens above it, has always been to me an inspiration—a solace, an uplifting of the scrap of heaven within me.

I cannot think that such a city is, indeed, passed away for ever; any more than I can believe that the gallant men who have died in its defence have run their earthly course. I know in my heart that that which matters—the soul of the city, the spirits of the undying Dead—remain with us everlastingly, to influence, maybe unconsciously, future generations to nobler purpose and less selfish enterprise. And, perchance, they who have died that our world may be clean and wholesome will be born again, to remould nearer to the heart's desire this sorry scheme of things when the gods have regained control.

I have seen Ypres at varying heights of from 18,500 to 200 feet. When far above, one sees what resembles brownish white rocks by the shore, after countless ages of buffeting by the waves; whilst the sea, having achieved its purpose, is filtering away in watercourses around and from its work of demolition. As one descends, it is noticed that here and there, the waves have failed in their mission of total disintegration. Still lower it is apparent that it is not rocks but the abodes of men that have been maltreated. When as low as one can conveniently venture, it is easy to discern the skeletons of stately piles. Of the renowned cathedral, a tapering remnant remains where once a noble spire pointed to the skies; and of that triumph of architecture, the Cloth Hall, three scarred and bespattered sides stand out massive, grim and forbidding.

Streets once bordered by happy homes are flanked by fragments of brick and mortar hastily shoved aside that armies may be maintained and fed. Acres are levelled as if by the wheels of God, or a procession of monstrous tank juggernauts. Vegetation, decaying and lifeless in winter, verdant and progressive in summer, is extending over the unfertile soil, For the rest, shell holes, ruins, water—such is Ypres of today. Only here and there a gaunt and limbless tree serves to remind us of gardens, lovers, and romance of bygone days and our problematical future.

We crossed the lines and flew over desolate country towards where, the map informed me, "Westroosebeke" once stood. As is his custom, Archie hurled innumerable projectiles at the formation. Personally, I did not hear a single burst, but it was evident that the rear machines were having a tempestuous voyage.

Swerving to the left, we made for Staden, where the gunners distributed their favours impartially. *"Wouff! Wouff!"* Archie is getting unpleasant. *"Crunch! Crunch!"*—his unpleasantness has arrived. It is consolatory to realise that, by the time the report is heard, all danger is past from that particular shell. The barrage being exceptionally heavy, D—— steered an irregular course, climbed and lost height, and we came to no harm. It is doubtful, however, if it is advisable for individual pilots to take upon themselves the onus of dodging Archie. The leader and his observer can see what is going on and can act accordingly, when all machines should follow, keeping strictly in formation.

Independent action results at the best in the disorganisation of the patrol for combined offensive purposes; and, at the worst, in the isolation of a single machine upon which all guns will concentrate—as well as Huns in the air. In practice it has been found that the chances of Archie bringing down a single machine are infinitely greater than of bagging one of a formation. This is, presumably, due to the fact that Gunners are inclined to aim at the latter as a whole instead of selecting one of its number and steadily haunting it.

The German Flying Corps were out today in greater force than usual, Specks miles away unattended by black puffs were immediately classified as hostile. Fifteen black midgets coming from the north-east were growing larger every moment. In those days practically the only enemy fighting aeroplane met with at high altitudes was the Albatross Scout—two-seaters were seldom encountered at over 10,000 feet. All British fighting machines, with the exception of the Sopwith Camel—which differs from all others, whether Ally or enemy—had dihedral; which means that both right and left wings inclined downwards towards their junction with the body of the machine.

There was no doubt that these graceful, birdlike creatures were Albatrii—to give the plural in the R.A.F. fashion. There was no mistaking the silhouette formed by the wings which, of equal length, are parallel with the horizontal. As they came still nearer, their peculiar V-shaped struts confirmed their type. They were flying on the same level as the bulk of our formation, namely 16,000 feet. Our leader was steadily climbing, hoping to gain the undoubted advantage of height. They did the same, with the result that the rapidly converging machines simply mingled together and a dogfight ensued in which everyone blazed away at any and every opponent within reasonable range. The German machines were painted with large, broad rings about their bodies. The predominant colours were green, brown and black, and it is probable that this was an example of "camouflage," for when flying between us and the ground, they merged into the landscape and were difficult to detect.

During the next few moments, I caught fleeting glimpses of machines diving and zooming; of tracer wisps; an of one black-crossed, graceful, harlequin-like bird spinning slowly to earth. My attention was necessarily concentrated on defending the tail and *taking* such opportunities as presented themselves for offensive action. D—— had, in the general *mêlée*, dived and fired on two occasions, but without putting a Hun out of action; and I had fired at a machine that, spitting bullets, approached unpleasantly near my tail. Shortly afterwards a Hun flew past at right angles to me pursued by one of our machines which, in its turn, had a Hun on its tail. The latter was diving at an angle of about 20 degrees and was rapidly overhauling our plane.

When within 150 yards of it, and about the same distance from us, I took aim with the ring sight and fired. The first few rounds were some feet in front, but directly in the course which was being taken. There was no necessity to alter the aim—hold the gun steady and nose and pilot must pass through the barrage. Streaks of fire entered the nose, then the fuselage, and finally the pilot's cockpit. It is probable that he was hit and fell forward on to the joystick, for the machine suddenly dived vertically. Almost at the same moment a wing fell off. I made no effort to watch the machine to earth. It was bound to crash and was in fact confirmed by an anti-aircraft battery as having done so.

One must learn to take such incidents—brim-full of excitement and interest—calmly. It was my first Hun and I was delighted. But in a dog-fight there is no time to moralise or philosophise over a single victim. There are others waiting to be shot down, and they are by no means unarmed antagonists whom one can disregard. I have one case in mind of a young and enthusiastic observer, who was so engrossed in watching his first (and last) Hun crash, that he was riddled with bullets without, in all probability, having seen the machine from which they came.

By this time some few of the Albatrii had been shot down and we had been reinforced by: two scouts. The enemy had been severely strafed and were making efforts to break off the combat. It was not advisable to follow them far, as a strong westerly wind was blowing—making it rash to venture further, lest our petrol should give out.

D—— had been taking (and making) opportunities, and was one of the last to speed the parting enemy. He dived on the rear machine, which very possibly was already damaged, and fired a few short bursts. The Hun dived vertically at terrific speed and disappeared far below in the ground mist. No effort was made to flatten out; so, we were, it is hoped, right in assuming that she was out of control.

The leader, having fired a number of red lights to collect the formation, we crossed the lines in rather scattered array and made for home. Here the C.O., as was his wont, awaited us on the aerodrome, and we gathered round him and reported. Seven Huns were claimed. Of these five were ultimately confirmed by independent observers as having crashed, and the remaining two could not be followed down to the earth owing to the ground-mist. Of those confirmed, the wings of two had folded back; one went down in a spinning nose dive; another stalled and turned over and over; whilst the fifth went down in a slow spin.

Twelve machines had set out. By ones and twos eleven returned—P—— and L—— were still out. Where are they? Did anyone see them go down? The questions were asked anxiously, but calmly, unexcitedly as if referring to the fate of an old umbrella. No satisfactory answer was forthcoming. They and their machine had just disappeared.

The sky that noticed all makes no disclosure,
And earth keeps up her terrible composure.

It is extraordinary how complacently, how composedly such incidents are taken by squadrons. Presumably it is a matter of usage—of familiarity. A "show" returns. A machine is "missing." It is—unless it has been seen to go down—expected to return in due course; or perhaps we may be informed by 'phone that a forced landing has been made. The hours go by, and in the absence of definite news one wonders what has happened to the pilot and observer. "Landed at —— for lunch, an old dodge of theirs," answers the optimist. Still no news. For a day there is a meagre hope. They may have landed far from a telephone. Then "Afraid they have bought it. Hell of a war, isn't it?" "Have a drink?"—followed by silence; a mute toast at dinner; hardly a reference.

Death is a common occurrence in these days—is incorporated in the scheme of things. We are all accustomed to it and we do not fear it—just take it—accept it as all in the day's work. As Gryffith Fairfax writes:—

DEATH in one day, by putting off his cloak
Of lonely terror, wherewith he went decked,
Has lost his old inscrutable aspect,
And treads familiar among fearless folk.

In this—our airmen's life—the days are happy ones. We live well, sleep well—have all the funds we reasonably need, the choicest of boon companions, no worries. Work—if so, it can be called—is a species of adventure. Every moment of a flight is of interest. There is the panorama below—the heavens above—the sun—the clouds—the other birds in the skies—the flight over world-famed battlefields—the lines—Archie—looking for Huns. There is the keen cold air—the sea in the distance—the floods—the canals and rivers—the towns and villages. All these and much besides have their moment's joy, wrested from Time the ever-swift. Added to this is the thrilling, pulsating life of a "scrap." Is this work? Is it not rather pure unadulterated adventure and romance? So, the life is a good one, and so it gives us heart to die manfully. No one seems to care whether he dies or no.

In our hearts of course we do care. Life is so sweet, so utterly sweet for us all. Can it be that there is something that has inspired our youth to look Death in the face unflinchingly, or have we become so inured to risks that it is a case of familiarity breeding contempt?

In the meantime, we live fiercely, preparatory to dying (if needs be) gamely.

CHAPTER 4

A Very Close Call

Some days after the events narrated in the last chapter my young and adventurous pilot D—— was due for home leave. We had become accustomed to one another's methods and eccentricities and the prospect of flying with another man did not appeal to me. I was to follow two days later to attend a ten days' course in the vicinity of London. Much, however, may happen in a couple of days—given good flying weather—as the incidents I am about to relate will prove. The pilot with whom one has become accustomed to fly may not be the Ace of all Aces, but you and he have shared in many exciting and eventful experiences, and you should have in one another—

The faith of men that have brothered men,
By more than easy breath.

Nothing is worse for an observer's nerves than to fly with a varied assortment of pilots—good, bad and indifferent. Co-operation between the occupants of a fighting-plane is essential, if their names are not to adorn the list of "Missing." The knowledge that his flying partner is stout and dependable goes very far towards inculcating confidence and enthusiasm in a beginner in aerial warfare.

Having seen D—— on to a squadron tender, *en route* for Boulogne, I meandered back to breakfast somewhat disconsolate, and for the first time not looking forward to the day's promise of adventure, I was to fly with a pilot: who had been over the lines twice only. He was considered an adept at handling a machine. This, however, was an attribute common to the great majority of pilots who, at this stage of the war, had been sent overseas. But only in actual war-flying can one learn the game as played in the sternest school.

Nothing but danger and fighting can prove whether any given man has the temperament—the cool head in emergency—without which he is doomed to failure in a Battle Squadron. All who challenge the Air Hun to combat *à outrance* have to buy their experience. During the paying stage their life hangs as by a thread; but after perhaps fifty hours of intense life over Hunland, that thread has become so stout a rope that only ill-luck or a chance shot can sever it.

It would be of interest to know how many airmen who have gone West have disappeared from our hospitable messes during their first month of war flying. The list would, I think, comprise a considerable percentage of our total Air Force casualties.

Flying in formation is an art in itself, involving as it does a sympathetic understanding of the use of the throttle by which speed is regulated. To be a crack flier the same qualities as are needed in horsemanship are required. At least, that is the opinion which I—a humble observer—have formed. The nearer the "hands" of a pilot approach to those of the rider of a Grand National Winner, the better; for, instinctively, they will then impart information to the brain concerning the moods, the vices and the virtues of the throbbing, pulsating creature they control. A perfect horseman should make an ideal pilot; for his hands, brain and eye would, one infers, work in complete sympathy with his machine.

New pilots find it by no means an easy thing to keep in formation, and the straggler is the *pièce de résistance* for which roving bands of Huns will travel far and fast. Members of a large formation may see only minute black specks far away; but if a single machine—from engine trouble or other cause—lags behind, it is astonishing how these midgets increase in size to the anxiously observant eyes of the occupants of the lonely plane.

Today I was destined to realise to the last degree the necessity for the advice so often given in aerial schools: "Keep in formation; don't straggle." The "show" was due to patrol east of the Boche lines from 11.0 to 12.30. At 10.15 twelve pilots and observers assembled at the office for the *pow-wow*. On proceeding to the machine in which we were detailed to fly, and of which my companion-to-be possessed some knowledge, we found that it was temporarily *hors de combat*, and had to fall back upon another. This did not increase my keenness for the morning's outing, as it meant that any idiosyncrasies it possessed would add to my pilot's perplexities.

We were in the "above guard" formation, *i.e.,* the group of three flying over and behind the main body to guard against surprise and to allow the remainder a fair field, free from molestation, when scrapping.

Today, instead of heading towards Ypres, *viâ* Poperinghe, the flight commander chose a course which we had seldom taken. Skirting the north-eastern edge of the Forest of Nieppe we left Hazebrouck on our left—alive with trains and reminiscent of a bomb raid, some evenings before, which had partially marred the enjoyment of an excellent dinner of which the outstanding features were fowls and Chambertin, supplied by our amiable hostess, Madame of Le Cheval Blanc. Thence to Bailleul, with its array of glass houses—destined to be shattered to bits a couple of months later—and following the railway line, we came to Armentiéres, already groaning under persistent bombardments, and bearing little resemblance to the cheery town of spies, Louis Roederer and tea shops of 1915.

We crossed the lines to the accompaniment of loud, strident, welcoming *"wouffs"* from Archie and followed the line of the Lys River to Comines and Wervicq. Our leader apparently wished to show his contempt for the anti-aircraft batteries located near the latter, for he calmly completed a tour of the town under dangerously accurate and concentrated fire. After we had headed north-east for a few minutes, our compass pointed due north, and we were flying about a mile to the left of and parallel with the Menin-Roulers road.

The leader was now at 14,000 feet or thereabouts, with the formation above him and to his rear, at heights up to 17,000 feet. Our correct position was on the right of the leader of the "Above Guard" formation, and we should have been at as great an altitude as any one; instead of which we were flying at 15,000 feet, and half a mile to the rear of the nearest machine. We were in the dubious position of being candidates for the belt of any "head hunter" that might be spoiling for a fight, or of roving patrols who preferred attacking a single machine to a strong formation.

The situation was a distinctly dangerous one and it is unfortunate that I did not advise the pilot to turn west and make for the lines and safety. Instead, I contented myself with passing him numerous notes telling him to make an effort to climb to his old place in the formation. This, presumably, he was unable to do, for he must have realised that by straggling we were courting disaster.

My mind flew back to my schooldays and the pathetic spectacle of a small boy reciting a certain famous passage from Vergil: *"Facilis descensus Averni est"*—*"Easy is the descent to Avernus, but to retrace thy steps and return to the upper air—that is the labour—that the toil,"* etc. A large-hearted classical-master would have me repeat this daily upon

"Bristol" Fighter, Type F2B, Rolls-Royce Engine

his arrival in our classroom; he had his gaze meditatively fixed upon the life career of his erratic and unstable pupil. In those good old days before the era of flight he expected me to end my days ingloriously. Prospects of sudden demise at the hands of Huns in the air had not then been dreamed of even by the most learned in classical mythology.

A red light fired from one of the foremost machines transferred me from the land of dreams to that of stern reality. In vain I searched the skies for enemy planes. No sooner had I assured myself that a false alarm had been given than the pilot put the nose of the machine down and dived steeply. Usually when diving on a Hun I have been able to overcome the intensified rush of air sufficiently to take an intelligent interest in passing events. Whether we were on this occasion diving at greater speed than usual I cannot say, but I was kept to a great extent glued to my seat. Consequently, I did not see the machine at which he was shooting, when *cac-cac-cac-cac-cac* informed me that he was getting busy. After firing a long burst, he pulled partially out of the dive and I caught a fleeting glimpse of the black crosses of an Albatross Scout diving to earth.

It occurred to me in a sudden, illuminating flash that all was not well with our machine. After diving and firing at the Hun I expected it to be flattened out. But this had not occurred—at least, not entirely. It was acting as if it were nose-heavy, for the tail was slightly above the horizontal. At the same time whilst making progress towards the west we seemed to be descending in slow spirals. After inclining downwards to the right for some distance, the machine would appear to go slowly for a few moments whilst deliberating on its next move. Its mind being made up, it would go through the same process to the left, after which came the incline to the right again, and soon. So far as I was able to judge from my limited knowledge of aeronautics we were out of control. There was nothing for me to do but to keep a sharp lookout for diving Huns—who, if they had noticed our predicament, would inevitably take an interest in the proceedings.

At the time I was not aware that a burst of fire had passed through the engine from the right front to the left rear. The injury had doubtless been inflicted by the Hun on whom we had dived. After a few moments of these erratic movements, it dawned upon me that it was only a matter of time before we crashed. I had a minute or two to live, just a brief breathing space between glorious life and—what? The yesterday's seven thousand years of dear old *infidel* Omar, or perchance life again on another planet? May the gods—if gods there be—place us on one like unto this, but in which wars do not claim us before we have tasted all its joys.

I have before remarked on the influence of the air of the upper regions which—in my opinion—makes men to a very great extent impervious to fear. Nerves are sooner or later developed by all who fly. But not for some time after they have made themselves felt on *terra firma* do they appear in actual flying. It is the anticipation of unpleasant incidents that generates fear. In contact with them all is forgotten in the struggle for self-preservation. So, for a time—later, when, metaphorically speaking, the nerve germs have bred sufficient white corpuscles to overcome the healthy red ones, fear begins to assert its sway when up aloft. The victim is now in a state of perpetual intense excitement, masked by an outward semblance of calm; and the wise and observant squadron commander decides that it is time another of his officers went to Home Establishment for a rest.

I am sure that men undergoing equal strain and suspense on the ground would not last so long. The infantry will probably not agree; but I, too, have been in the trenches, and have come to the conclusion that the actual nerve strain endured by them bears no comparison to that to which airmen are subjected. Remember in Fighting Squadrons (and it is to them that I refer) one goes over the top as it were once or twice on all except very "dud" days and sometimes three, four or more times.

Always there is the certainty of a vociferous welcome from Archie, and in most cases, there is a scrap; added to which there is the ever-present nightmare of engine trouble, with its visions of a forced landing on unsuitable and perhaps hostile ground, as well as the possibility of bad weather conditions. The strain is enormous, and I believe it is only some quality in the rarefied and purer air met with, that enables it to be borne for any appreciable time.

For some fateful seconds, one part of Me—the real Me—appeared to be detached from all that was happening, and to be looking on calmly, unconcernedly at the other part. It was as if my soul was gazing out at the feeble worldly exploits of its partner the body:

Why if the soul can fling the dust aside,
And naked on the air of heaven ride,
Were't not a shame, were't not a shame for him
In this clay carcass crippled to abide?

My thoughts in these absorbing moments have become indelibly impressed on my memory, in spite of the almost incredible swiftness with which they flashed through my brain. Strangely enough I was not haunted by ghosts of the past—by visions of times misspent and things undone. It would not have been surprising had it been so as wandering life in four continents is not conducive to the production of carpet-slippered angels. I felt regrets; but they were for joys untasted, love unproved, beauty unappreciated, for not having made the most of life, for not having squeezed from existence as much of real happiness as I might have done—and would, could the clock have been put back. In a flash much was revealed to me as to the secret of life—that money and possessions are as nought, and only happiness and love count. In this lay no new discovery; yet how few realise it before it is too late! From the jaws of death came the message—"Live and love."

Always on my journeyings in wars and through peaceful lands I have carried with me a small edition of Omar—which is to say that I have never lacked a friend. He—perhaps I should include FitzGerald and say they—understood the incoherent cry of the world for sympathy and understanding. No poet has so intelligently voiced the appeal for light upon what is dark—for a ray of hope upon what is difficult to understand. His doctrine "Unborn tomorrow and dead yesterday—why fret about *them* if today be sweet?" is pleasant enough in its way.

It provides at once an excuse and a justification for evil living. But its devil-may-care influence has played its part in undermining the morals of our youth in these war days, when whatever views may be held as to a future life, the prospect of unlimited tomorrows in this have been sadly discounted; but the lesson that was forced upon me apparently too late in the day embodied an extension of Omar's teaching.

A voice seemed to say:

There may or may not be a future, but whether there is or is not, the best spent life is that in which the greatest sum total of happiness is enjoyed. In your past breathless, restless career have you searched for this boon where it is most likely to be found? Have you not rather stirred the muddy depths? Have you not sought out and pursued the fleeting phantom joys, which leave no milestones on Life's highway on which to look back with satisfaction? Quiet rest, peace of mind and mental alertness give more lasting joy than the consuming energy which, mistaking the shadow for the substance, reaches out selfish hands for passing pleasure. The search for happiness should supersede that for wealth and for renown; and it is not in the slime, in the sordid byways of cities, but in comparative solitude with the mind, with friends, with love, that it is most likely to be found.

Thus was I informed that whilst I had lived it was not in the manner most conducive to happiness. Then came other thoughts—that it is better for those who play at this game to be single so that a bullet passes through one only.

I was recalled from fleeting considerations of the might-have-been to more mundane matters. The erratic movements ceased as it is hoped will the Great War—as suddenly as it began. (This was written prior to the Armistice). Whether this was due to the juggling of the pilot with the engine and controls or to luck I have no idea. Once more we were flying straight. Our altitude was 6,000 feet, and our formation was disappearing towards the north, whilst we were luckily heading towards the lines. Four Albatross Scouts who had been hovering above us now appeared, diving on our tail.

They were from 100 to 150 yards away and firing steadily. Circular wisps of tracer smoke were preceding their machines, whilst occasional flashes of light from speeding bullets gave rough indications of the degree of skill in marksmanship possessed by our pursuers. This proved to be surprisingly mediocre, for only a few bullets vented the fuselage in my vicinity. Having flattened out they sat on our tail and continued the strafing process.

In the meantime, I had not been idle; I had fired a full magazine at one machine as it dived, but without noticeably damaging it. To account for a 'plane diving steeply is one of the most difficult things in the world, as sporting readers, with remembrances of the woods and driven birds late in the season, will readily realise. It was necessary to shoot nearly vertically upwards. On quiet sober reflection some days afterwards, I came to the conclusion that, of the four machines, I had singled out the one which offered the hardest if most sporting shot. The others were diving less steeply and therefore presented easier targets.

After changing magazines, I concentrated on the nearest Hun, firing directly at his nose—an easy shot as he was flying dead level. After firing fifty to sixty rounds smoke commenced to issue from his tail and his nose inclined downwards. I gave him the remaining rounds, exchanged magazines, and found only three machines left. Hastily sighting on another, I poured a stream of lead and fire into him, but was diverted from this by the sudden appearance of another scout. At one moment he was diving steeply on us from my left front; at the next he was flashing past my tail, and so adjacent that there was little space between our wing tip and his. Evidently, he had dived and fired a burst without success; now he offered a comparatively easy shot. I swung the gun round and fired instinctively, as if my Lewis were a shot gun.

There was no time for thought or calculation; the scout was rushing past at 200 miles per hour and only for a long second was he within my zone of fire. At point-blank range tracers can be relied upon. I pulled the trigger and streaks of fire entered the fuselage a foot or so behind the pilot. Remedying the error, I fired again. After three rounds the gun stopped. The magazine was empty and the Hun had escaped.

I put on another magazine and devoted my attention to the nearest of the attackers. Once more after a few rounds there was an ominous silence. I applied immediate action, pulled back the cocking handle and pressed the trigger. No welcome response rewarded my efforts. The gun had jammed. To endeavour to right matters with three persistent gunners endeavouring to shoot one down is distinctly disconcerting. I tapped the pilot on the head and pointed to the gun with the object of informing him that it was out of action. In return he pointed to the hole through the engine, thereby implying that he could do nothing except make for the lines. This he was already doing, whilst throwing the machine about considerably, to make it more difficult for our pursuers to hit us.

For a moment, my gaze had wandered from them; now to my astonishment, delight, and relief I saw that one and all had just completed a turn, and were making back over Hunland. German machines, owing to our acknowledged and indisputable superiority in the air, do not relish crossing our lines. They had chased us as far as they dared to come. Nevertheless, it was an extraordinarily lucky chance that we reached the safety zone just when our prospects looked exceedingly gloomy.

Below us lay the tortuous windings of the trenches and in front Zillebeke Lake—than which it would be hard to name a landmark more useful for flying men. This sheet of water, triangular in shape, has the apex pointing, if not directly due east, at least as nearly so as is necessary for practical purposes; it can be seen for many miles and on innumerable occasions pilots and observers, when in doubt as to their whereabouts, have hailed it with delight.

Our engine was in a parlous state. We had come down out of control from 14,000 feet and had crossed the lines at 6,000 feet. We were now gliding down, having switched off the engine.

A forced landing was plainly indicated. To land on unknown country is always a hazardous undertaking. To do so on. the unwholesome, pock-marked, sponge-like area of the Ypres salient is an escapade which at the best means more work for aeroplane workers in Coventry and elsewhere, and at the worst ... well, it's a common occurrence. Hardly less inviting was the conglomeration of huts and makeshift residences of the immediate "front behind the front," between which were scattered here and there plots of unoccupied ground of inconsiderable size.

One of these the pilot eventually selected as his landing ground. It was by no means an ideal one, being only about 130 yards in length and bordered on all sides by huts. A risky spot, but quite legitimate for an experienced pilot. Taking precautions, however, I sat tightly down; holding on grimly to the framework of the cockpit, with my knees braced firmly under the magazines. I hardly expected to crash on landing but was extremely dubious as to the pilot's ability to pull the machine up before it crashed into a building. Looking through the camera hole in the fuselage the ground came nearer and nearer until a very slight vibration was noticeable as the wheels struck the ground. Then followed an appreciable pause. The next thing I knew was that bloody, dusty and aching, I was on my hands and knees some yards away.

The landing had been a bad one. The machine had pitched on to its nose and I had been hurled out. As I attempted to stand up, the tail, following me over, hit me lightly on the back and sent me down again. I raised myself on to my knees, and with difficulty stood up and gazed around in bewilderment.

Troops from all quarters rushed up, amongst them some officers of a famous English line regiment. The pilot was none the worse for the crash. I was somewhat bruised and sore; and, although a strong brandy peg helped to mend matters, it was six weeks before I emerged from a cure at Etaples and Paris-Plage.

45

CHAPTER 5

Twenty Four Hours of Action

When I returned to the squadron, ready for another spell of flying, I had missed the great retreat towards Amiens. Our squadron, although some way distant, sent machines daily to bomb and machine-gun the advancing enemy. This was by no means new work for the R.A.F., but never had it been undertaken on such a large scale. One result of this ground strafing offensive was to "put the wind up" the Hun to such an extent that never since has he exposed his troops so recklessly to our attacks. Pilots and observers told me of gorgeous targets: whole battalions on the march; roads full of transport and guns; troops massing for attack. On these they dropped bombs, causing indescribable panic and great losses, whilst the fire of machine-guns caused innumerable casualties.

But if the material results were considerable, the most important factor was the effect on the enemy's morale. Day by day and night by night he was never immune from molestation by our machines. There was always the possibility of throbbing engines overhead, with the uncertainty as to the movements of the pilots. On the march, in billets, in the mess, when lying down at night—always was there the ever-present fear of aircraft. I have yet to meet the man who can disregard bombing attacks. Their cumulative effect on the nerves cannot be overestimated. The material damage inflicted by raids may be, and perhaps often is, slight, but they are a very potent factor in persuading an army of the blessings of Peace. Never was there better Peace propaganda than bombing.

At this time, however, although the Air Force had their "tails up" and held the ascendancy in the air, our fortunes as a whole were at a low ebb. We had known that the Hun was going to attack in the spring, and our job was plain—namely, to hold him up until the arrival of sufficient Americans to turn the scale. If we could succeed the war would eventually be won by the Allies. If we could not, and the Germans took Paris and overran much of France, capturing vast armies, then, whilst knowing that defeat for us was impossible—however, it is best not to think of unpleasant contingencies.—The enemy was eventually held, and the sequel is known to the world. The part played by our squadrons in holding up and ultimately staying the advance on Paris has, I think, been recognised by the infantry, and we can ask for nothing better than the knowledge that we were able to help them in critical days.

On my return to the squadron in the early days of April the enemy's initial onslaught had been checked and it was problematical; where he would next attack. On the night of April 7, he heavily shelled our front from Lens to Armentiéres. On the morning of the 9th he recommenced, and after a bombardment of the greatest intensity his attack was launched, in a dense fog, some three hours later.

The weather has invariably helped the enemy, whilst we in our attacks have often been unfortunate. An exceptionally dry spring had prepared the ground for an advance, and for two days impossible atmospheric conditions had hampered our Air Service. During the greater part of the April "Push," low-lying clouds, storms and fogs, virtually put the Air Service out of action, and there were few opportunities of locating and breaking up his massed attacks, or for obtaining information as to his dispositions and movements.

Throughout the morning and the greater part of the afternoon of the 9th thick fogs prevented observation, and we could do nothing but remain inactive, listening to the shell-fire which with greater or less intensity continued without a break. Towards evening the fog lifted slightly, and we were sent to fly over Laventie and Fleurbaix and bomb and shoot up enemy troops. Our bombs were dropped on Fleurbaix, in the streets of which we discerned and shot up some Hun infantry. The next day we were out of action again, and on the 11th only three machines, of which ours was one, went out to reconnoitre the battlefront, flying at 1,000 feet with the clouds immediately above us.

The 12th turned out fine and clear, and it is of my adventures on that day that I propose to write.

I cannot call to mind twenty-four hours in which I have crowded more exciting and eventful occurrences. In addition to making four daylight war flights, we flew for the first and last time at night and crashed the machine, after which we were bombed by the German Flying Corps.

The first "show" was a bombing and machine-gunning expedition to Steenwerck, which had been taken by the Germans on the evening of the 10th. After being called at 5.30 a.m. we drank a cup of hot tea and set off. Each machine carried a bomb, for delivery on town or station. Our objective was distant about twelve miles. There was no need to climb, so we made straight for it *viâ* Caestre, Flêtre, Meteren and Bailleul. The sun had by now dispelled the low-lying mists and gave promise of a fine spring day. Fields below, in February brown or black, day by day were putting on their spring mantle of green, whilst pastureland was awakening to new life. Rivers and watercourses sparkled and glittered in the sunshine. All nature was awakening to the call of the spring. The sap was rising in meadow, field and creature, and yet it was decreed that on this glorious day we should fly on a pilgrimage of destruction—to destroy life and the habitat of life.

We passed over Caestre, teeming with railway life, and followed the road to Flêtre and Meteren and thence on to Bailleul, 1½ to 2 miles south of which the German Armies were temporarily held up. We crossed the lines and noted that Archie had not yet been brought up. "*Cac-cac-cac*" from below informed us that machine-guns were busy on us and holes appeared in our wings. Of enemy aircraft there was no sign. We had hoped to have encountered troops on the march, or transport, but on this trip, we were unfortunate.

Over the town we released our bombs, and clouds of smoke and debris from buildings and the sound of explosions followed. We could only hope that we had been lucky and inflicted damage on personnel. We continued flying south for some distance, but meeting with no suitable target for our machine-guns, turned back and made for the trenches. The Huns on seeing us approach ducked and took what cover they could. D—— dived from 150 to 50 feet, firing assiduously the while, and then zoomed up and gave me a chance with the rear gun. This he did four times until, with a small supply of ammunition left for defensive purposes in case enemy aircraft should be encountered he steered for home.

On our return we breakfasted, and prepared for an Offensive Patrol at 9.30. We did not go on this, however, as the C.O. was informed over the 'phone that the army commander wished to know if Hun cavalry were, as had been reported, in the Forest of Nieppe. This is a large expanse of woodland, by far the largest forest over which we were in the custom of flying; being perhaps twice, the size of battle-scarred Houthulst—its maximum length is 4 miles, and it is approximately 3½ miles from north to south. Snugly ensconced in it is the little village of La Motte, the simple dwellers in which have doubtless been from time immemorial devoted adherents of the old *seigneurs* living in the noble *château* about which their cottages cluster. Foresters' houses are scattered at intervals alongside the numerous shooting roads which intersect in regular and parallel lines this venerable domain of the old French aristocracy.

D—— and I were detailed to fly over and report as to the presence or otherwise of enemy advanced patrols.

We wasted no time in setting off and headed straight for the forest, over which we steered an irregular course until perfectly satisfied that the enemy were nowhere in possession. Flying at 200 feet, there was no difficulty in discerning all movement. All we found was a few deserted tents, a number of straggling troops resting and cooking in the vicinity of the *château*, and some peasants fleeing with their worldly possessions from the momentarily victorious Hun. Our report was telephoned to the army within twenty-five minutes of having received our orders.

The role of the Air Force is the obtaining of information, and this was a startling example of the reformation the era of flying has effected in the branch of the service known as Intelligence. The distance to the centre of the forest from the aerodrome was roughly 10 miles. Thus, we had accomplished without any possibility of mistake and without risk in twenty-five minutes what in the days of scouting by cavalry could only have been done in three or four hours, and then with difficulty and danger.

At twelve o'clock we accompanied five other machines on another bombing expedition to Steenwerck. We flew at 2,000 feet. *En route*, a number of white bursts around three specks far above gave us the information that the Huns were today displaying unusual temerity, and were giving our Archie gunners opportunities for target practice.

There was no sign of life in the town or station of Steenwerck. The Hun had by now learned the advisability of taking cover on the approach of aircraft. We dropped our bombs on the station and hoped for the best; after which, in the absence of a definite target, we sprayed the station yard and buildings with bullets and, picking up the remainder of the formation, headed for home.

In the afternoon we were detailed for a reconnaissance; "I" required information as to the enemy's intentions. Our reserves were by no means large, and, to be used to the best advantage, they must be at hand where an attack appeared imminent. We were instructed to pay special attention to roads leading towards Merville, and then to reconnoitre the country south of Bailleul. The latter town was still held by our troops, who were being hard pressed. Of the six machines, ours and another were to fly low, whilst the others remained above as escort. Thus, two observers would be enabled to study the country in comparative security.

Always when crossing the lines, we carried a bomb. On this occasion the straggling little town of Neuf Berquin had been selected as our objective. So as to be free for the more important work of obtaining information we made straight for it and "dropped our egg." A few Huns were sighted; but the object of a reconnaissance is to obtain information, not to scrap. In fact, it may be said that the *raison d'être* of the R.A.F. is to get knowledge of the enemy's movements whilst preventing him from learning ours.

We were now free to devote our attention to road movement, whilst at the same time keeping a lookout for hostile aircraft, in spite. of machines protecting us. Visibility was fairly good. Roads could be seen for a considerable distance. We flew over the Lys midway between. Estaires and Merville. At intervals were distinctly seen motor transport drawn up alongside the road. South of the river a closer scrutiny revealed infantry lining the ditches on either side. They did not fire upon us, so it may be assumed that orders had been given to make every effort at concealment and not to invite attention. For us the opportunity was too good to be lost, and we went low down and took turns at spraying the ditches.

Seeing they had been detected, a group of twenty or more commenced to shoot at us, whereupon the fire was taken up by all as we passed by. This fortunately enabled me to get a better idea of the number of troops moving towards Merville. Foolishly to allow ourselves to be shot down unnecessarily was far from our thoughts; nor were we out to shoot up the enemy's troops. Our object was to obtain information; and whilst at times a fight is necessary to achieve one's purpose, it is not justifiable to take risks which might endanger the safe delivery of intelligence. Therefore, we climbed again to a position of reasonable safety.

Having noted mentally the approximate numbers of men and lorries on this road, we turned south from Merville and found that troops were also being moved up from Locon, and were distributed at intervals—taking cover on our approach—for 4 to 5 miles.

If no further information was forthcoming, at any rate we congratulated ourselves on having news of importance for the army.

Roads leading towards Bailleul had now to be reconnoitred. These all appeared to be deserted. To make sure we came down to 200 feet, and, rather sooner than we anticipated, were flying over the German front line. "*Cac-cac-cac-cac*"—the enemy's machine-gunners opened a merry fusillade, which was punctuated by the intermittent crack of innumerable rifles. A lucky shot might at any moment send us crashing to earth. How we got away without a scratch is a marvel. The engine was not damaged; but the wings and fuselage, with fifty-three bullet holes, caused us to realise on our return how near we had been to "buying it."

Somewhere to our left our companion reconnaissance machine was going through the same ordeal. It received more punctures than ours, many of which penetrated to the engine, with the result that the machine had to be written off as unfit for further service. The pilot contrived to land safely, however, and the observer handed in much useful information.

By way of retaliation, I blazed away at the upturned faces, levelled rifles and spitting machine-guns. Before I could get off many rounds, we had passed over them and were looking down upon friendly uniforms. We passed over our front line and found our troops feverishly digging a new line of trenches covering Bailleul, and extending along the high ground known as the Ravelsburg Heights.

We made for home, landed, and reported to the intelligence officer. One of our escorting machines that had disappeared mysteriously when over Hunland had not returned. Some weeks later we heard that the pilot had been hit in the ankle by a bullet, and the machine had come down out of control. On crashing, no further injury was sustained by either occupant. As they were flying far above us, it gives one furiously to think on the mutability of Fate—that we should pass unscathed through thousands of leaden messengers, whilst they should be brought down by a chance shot at extreme range.

It had been a strenuous day. All pilots and observers had been four times to look at the war. Machines had been dropping bombs on, and firing ammunition at, many and varied targets—which, unfortunately, had not been so large as they were on the Somme in the previous month. This, at least, goes to prove that the work done in those stirring days had not been in vain. Their moral effect must have been incalculable, and such as to influence very greatly the success of any attack launched in fine, clear weather. Throughout the day we had been surmising that, owing to the advance of the enemy, it might become imperative for us to vacate our aerodrome and occupy another farther removed from active operations.

That we had not yet been shelled out was looked upon as in the nature of an oversight on the part of the German Command. We confidently expected to be the objective of a bombing raid during the night. Indeed, a Hun machine flying over us at 20,000 feet had, in all probability, been taking photographs with this end in view. Suddenly, all conjecture was set at rest, and the order came to fly west at once to an aerodrome about 10 miles away. Hurriedly we packed up; leaving the bulk of our luggage to be brought on by the transport, D—— and I squeezed a suitcase apiece into my cockpit, and, by the time the engine had been tuned up, we were ready to take off. The name of the village near which the aerodrome was situated was given us, and we started at once, in the wake of other machines.

It was just commencing to get dusk. The sun had, on its setting, left a faint red effulgence, towards which, our course being westwards, we now flew. Never before had D—— or myself been up at night. It was a new experience and we welcomed it; and, as is so often the case, realised not till afterwards the danger of the situation. It could not fail to be, if not dark, at least extremely dim and shadowy before we reached our destination. D—— had to land on an aerodrome unknown to him; and even with the help of flares, a first night-landing—like a first solo—is not without an element of risk. But of such thoughts we were, luckily, entirely free.

The romance appealed to us. Like the Athenians, we felt joy in doing "some new thing." Nor was the element of humour lacking. The sight of his "perfectly good observer" sitting like a monkey on our suitcases, with head and shoulders far out of the machine, aroused D—— to derisive scornful laughter. The thought of any trouble had not occurred to him. In the event of the machine turning over on landing my chances were absurdly small; and in a bad crash there were vast possibilities.

On climbing to a couple of thousand feet we found that the sky was full of machines. Other squadrons were on the move. In the dim light it was hard to distinguish one type from another; soon it became impossible. Those of our own squadron rapidly disappeared, and we were left to carry on as well as we could with rather a vague idea as to where we were going.

It was now getting darker every minute. The uncanny weirdness of the affair struck me forcibly. We seem so puny, so insignificant in the scheme of things. This, my one night flight, brought home to me very impressively my own littleness. It stirred my soul deeply. I have seen the sun rise over Mount Everest and have felt puny, a mere bubble. So, it was now. To those who scoff at the idea of a Supreme Power I recommend night flying. Then, more than by day, the grim solemnity of everything affects one with a feeling of awe, with an uncanny influence.

I felt that I was—not only now, but always—at the mercy of—what? I cannot say—but of some power, the extreme might of which can be very dimly conceived only when gazing o'er vast spaces on sea or land—at mighty mountains—at the greatest works of Nature.

It was getting still darker. We had passed by a large forest—that of Clairmarais—black and mysterious. An aerodrome lay at its edge. Numerous lights were being fired from the ground to direct wandering night birds; whilst flares, brilliantly burning, lit up the landing place. Figures, grotesque and fantastical, mingled with planes landing and landed.

There appeared to be some confusion; landing here would have been a perilous enterprise. Next day we heard of the crashes—quite a number—with luckily no loss of life, but some damage to limb. We conferred together and decided to go on—if not to our objective, at least to St. Omer, where a large aerodrome is situated.

Leaving the forest to our right, we passed over the flooded area, which lay reflecting remnants of light—calm and sullen in placid repose. St. Omer, dimly lighted and shadowy, was next reached. In its environs south-west of the town lay the aerodrome on which we proposed to land. Others had evidently already arrived there; and for the benefit of those following on, Very lights were being fired at frequent intervals. Flares were conspicuous by their absence. At one moment the surface of—the aerodrome was lit up brilliantly—at the next, it was correspondingly dark. D—— circled round preparatory to landing and, noting the direction of the wind, switched the engine off and glided down.

By now it had occurred to me that the landing was fraught with great possibilities. Of the other machines that had made for this aerodrome, very probably some had crashed. There was the danger of running into them. Then the perfunctory lighting up of the ground was deceptive to a pilot landing on unknown soil. Furthermore, perched as I was above suitcases, there was little chance for me if the machine should determine to turn turtle.

Still gliding down, there suddenly loomed up to our front a huge mound—apparently a rifle-range. Looking down we seemed to be missing it by inches. It reminded me of the Hill of Isandhlwana ("The Place of the Little Hand") in Zululand, where the British Forces sustained a serious reverse in 1879, and which I had passed close to when trekking through hostile country at night, with one companion, on the way to join a column operating against the modern Zulu in 1906. D—— opened the throttle and made another tour of the ground. By this time lights were going up in sufficient numbers. We landed slightly faster than usual. The machine made one prodigious hop, came to earth again and collapsed, with undercarriage in a hopeless muddle, propeller smashed to atoms—and, as we were informed the next morning, the machine as a whole quite beyond repair.

Our adventures were not yet over. There being no accommodation on the aerodrome, we took a tender and made for St. Omer, where we engaged beds and ordered dinner at our favourite hotel. The meal was proceeding merrily, the cooking was good and *vin rouge* abundant, when lights were switched off. This could mean one thing only—the approach of hostile bombing machines. We "carried on" by the aid of candles, whilst the whirr of engines overheard could be distinctly heard. The raiders appeared in no hurry to drop their "eggs."

They had probably a definite target, *e.g.*, the station. If so, their sense of location was erratic, for bombs were dropped promiscuously in many parts of the town. For a time, none came near us, but when we had congratulated ourselves that the raid was over there was a deafening report, and all the windows of our room were shattered by concussion from a bomb that demolished a house about 50 yards away.

The squadron pianist at this juncture proceeded to the piano and hammered out the opening chord of *A Perfect Day*. This was taken up by all until the rafters rang with the refrain, "*When you come to the end of a perfect day, and you sit,*" etc., etc.

The Hun had by now exhausted his supply of "hate," and was making his way homewards. As he did not return during the night a long sleep between sheets, followed by a hot bath, made ample amends for a day of strenuous endeavour.

CHAPTER 6

The Great German Offensive

During the German onslaught in the Armentiéres area in April the R.A.F. was, to a very great extent, out of action. On only three or four days was really fine weather experienced, during the three weeks which elapsed before the attacks of the enemy were brought to a standstill by the gallantry of the infantry and gunners. It is idle to speculate on the course of events, if, by a wave of the hand, we could, after the first day's retirement have dispelled the fogs and mists that prevailed so persistently.

At least we should have had great opportunities. The enemy would not have been able to march troops up by daylight, and deliver surprise attacks when and where he wished. His movements would have been continually under observation, which is to say that the R.A.F. would have played their part. Whilst fighting in the air appeals to the public as the work of "gallant gentlemen," its object is to enable equally "gallant gentlemen" on less good machines to do that for which the Force exists—namely, the supplying of information, whether by photography, reconnaissance, or by reporting to the gunners the bursts of shells.

Thirty to forty or more Huns shot down in one day is no small achievement; but to a large extent it is useless if, in spite of such losses, the enemy has been enabled to prevent our reconnaissance and artillery machines from carrying out their work. However, during these very critical days, weather conditions relieved the Bosche of the necessity for making ineffectual attempts to disorganise the eyes of the army.

I find on reference to my diary that, from the 9th April, when the German, offensive commenced, to the 30th, by which date it had spent its strength, only three days were suitable for our normal flying programme. Of the remaining nineteen days, ten were so atrocious that no flying at all was done, and on the others only extreme urgency warranted the sending out of one or more machines. It is of these expeditions that I am about to write. Two outstanding features were common to them all—execrable weather conditions and cool, resourceful piloting.

On the morning of April 16, Wytschaete was held by us in spite of renewed enemy attacks on the previous day. At midday six machines were ordered out to bomb and shoot up German troops who had been reported as massing for an attack in a small wood northeast of the village. D—— and I were of the six pilots and observers chosen. The weather was admittedly atrocious. On the expedition no other machines, friendly or hostile, were encountered. The mist lay at about 500 feet, and the outward journey promised to be swift-winged, owing to the added impetus given by a 30-mile-per-hour wind. Each machine took a single 112 lb. bomb and as much machinegun ammunition as could be conveniently carried.

Our objective being in detail unknown to us, D—— and I decided to fly to Ypres, and then follow the canal to its intersection with a road which made one of four cross roads, 600 yards to the east of which lay the wood. After a "bumpy" passage we reached Ypres and followed the canal to the south. The remnants of a bridge indicated where the road we recognised had once been. Three years, shelling had almost obliterated it, and it was with difficulty that we found our way.

We had considered that 90 seconds' flying should bring us to the cross-roads from the bridge. Before arriving there, however, we could dimly see the wood—or what was left of it; only distorted, limbless trunks remained. Realising the object of our mission I fingered my machine-gun expectantly. We were flying at 200 to 300 feet, and had an uninterrupted view downwards. Not a Hun was in sight except an unfortunate one who, propped against a tree, was sleeping his last sleep.

Field gunners, who could not have seen our machine, now let loose at us, shooting on sound. A single gun started, and in a few moments, it was taken up by every available gun of small calibre in the vicinity. White bursts of shrapnel were most numerous. Their "wouf" was of an infinitely less vociferating nature than that of Archie, and we paid little attention to what could only be erratic shooting. One hole, however, was made through the canvas of my cockpit large enough to have given me a trip home had the missile found me in its course.

Although we had, at some point or other, crossed the German lines, it was noteworthy that we had not been shot at from the ground.

This was perhaps due to the fact that, the range of vision being so, small, no time was given for riflemen and machine-gunners to awaken to the situation before we were once more shrouded in mist.

We returned by the same way that we had come and found that Wytschaete had been taken by the Huns some hours before. All of which tends to prove that we are fine-weather birds.

Since early morning we had stood by for a "show." Low-lying clouds had effectually debarred us, so far, from active participation in the war going on continuously a few minutes' flight away.

At 2.30 three machines, including ours, were ordered to reconnoitre the neighbourhood east of Strazeele Station where it was believed the enemy were massing for an attack. Strazeele Village—a pile of ruins—and Strazeele Station a mile farther south were both in our hands, with the Huns 1,000 to 2,000 yards away. Three and a half miles distant lay the great railway centre of Hazebrouck; although under fire from his guns, the Bosche would doubtless have liked it to be entirely his possession. We set off with the usual bomb and some hundreds of rounds of ammunition. The clouds lay at 800 to 1,000 feet. On climbing through them our altimeter showed 1,300 feet. Below us lay a gorgeous panorama. Of the earth we had just left there was no sign.

As far as the eye could reach it was screened from view by a barrier of pure white cloud-forms.

At greater heights I have often looked down upon spectacles more awe-inspiring in their picturesque grandeur—upon scenes far eclipsing that of today in massiveness. The particular charm of the present *vista* lay in the apparent modesty and alluring attractiveness of a type of celestial beauty which captivated whilst holding itself aloof. No mighty mountains reared their giant peaks heavenwards. No shaded valleys enclosed turbid rivers. Instead, intermingling with one another, were millions and still countless billions of semicircular forms, all of the purest virginal white. To describe the beauty of the clouds is, for me, quite impossible. I await impatiently the advent of the "Poet of the Air." One day he will—he must—appear.

Our two companion machines, outlined against this virginal background, showed up in silhouette like the Indian *sambhur* stag against the eastern dawn. Above us at 4,000 feet reposed the heavens' reserve of clouds—a dark, dirty, muddy surface, saturated with moisture hovering above, ever ready to pour its secretions on the temporary creation below—a grim reflection of the mutability of the beauty that passes. On reaching Hazebrouck the upper *strata* had risen; and the lower, after having split up into numerous particles, had passed into nothingness.

Following the railway line to Strazeele, we passed over the station at 1,000 feet and continued on over the German lines. At this time there was no German anti-aircraft battery in this sector. Our passage, therefore, was a comparatively peaceful one, as we were too high for machine-gun and rifle fire to hope for success, except by a chance shot. We followed the railway line for a couple of miles. No troops could be seen. Turning north, we reconnoitred Oursteen and Merris and from there flew south again to Vieux Berquin. It was evident that there was no attack imminent. Unfortunately, there was no prospect of the target for which an airman craves—massed troops in the open.

Estaires had been chosen as a target on which to drop our bombs in the absence of a more interesting mark. Following the leader, we climbed to 3,000 feet and, arriving over the centre of the town, at a signal from him despatched our missiles on their journey of destruction—of life, material, and morale—and especially the latter. The leader led us back again to the enemy country opposite St. Strazeele. Observation was now becoming difficult, as the clouds had again sprung up, apparently from nowhere. Only through gaps could the ground be seen.

In the hope of obtaining useful information, he commenced a tour of the trenches, following the line to Meteren and north of Bailleul to south of Kemmel Hill, which vantage point was still held by the Allies—actually, I think, by French troops. At this point dense low-lying clouds had completely obliterated the landscape. Being some distance in the rear of the formation when the leader suddenly dived into the clouds, we were, effectually separated from him and were left on our own. Underestimating the strength of the westerly wind we continued on for a few minutes longer; and then D——, putting his nose down, dived through the clouds. We came out at 200 feet. I could pick up no landmark that I knew. It took very few moments to realise that we were over enemy country.

Below were German guns, transport and men in a state of indescribable confusion. The countryside was desolate, bleak, and a mass of shell holes. Buildings were one and all level with the earth. Trees were limbless, roads scarcely discernible. D—— at once turned west, and we moved 16 *annas*—to use an Anglo-Indian phrase. For some minutes we flew on, all at sea. Presently we passed over a lake which appeared vaguely familiar. At first, I thought it must be that of Dickebusch; but, on looking again, found that it was much too small. Our line had, a day or two before, been withdrawn in the Ypres salient; it seemed to me that we must be flying over part of the evacuated area. Hastily glancing at the map, I found the lake we had just passed staring me in the face marked *"Etang de Bellewaurde."* In a few seconds Zillebeke Lake came into view, followed by Ypres itself. We arrived home with only a few bullet holes in the machine, but with a new realisation of the facility with which, in "dud" weather, one can lose one's way and—peradventure—one's freedom.

★★★★★★★★★★★★★★★★

Once more it was a day upon which, in the ordinary course, flying would not be considered. Not so in these times. The Bosche was— pushing persistently. Doubtless he thanked his gods for the mantle of a fog which it had pleased them to throw o'er the battle zone. It was the enemy who possessed the initiative in these early spring days. He had the men and the guns, enabling him to push when and where he wished. Not only this, but his plans were vastly simplified owing to his being able to move his troops by day without fear of detection; and, in many cases, to mass for attack a few hundred yards from our trenches without his object being revealed.

The army had, apparently, reason to believe that an attack was contemplated at 10.45 am. D—— and I were ordered to reconnoitre the line from the Forest of Nieppe to Meteren. Incidentally we were informed that a rival Squadron had attempted to get a view of this line, but had returned. It was obvious that we must make a success of the mission. It had rained and snowed at intervals since daybreak; for the moment, however, conditions were slightly more suitable. Nevertheless, the fog lay at 400 to 500 feet, enabling us to see barely to the end of the aerodrome. In addition, the countryside was being swept by a strong wind, which, 35 miles per hour on the ground, was gaining velocity with every foot of altitude.

D—— taxied our machine out, and turning so as to face the wind, opened the throttle and we took off. It was at once evident that the wind was a decidedly treacherous one. The machine shivered and shook like a colt on being first mounted. First one wing would go up, then the other; after this would come a succession of bumps. I had never flown under such damnable conditions, and every moment I expected we would go crashing to earth. However, D—— held to his course and no praise can be too high for his performance. At times fleecy wisps of vapour would envelop us, and we were momentarily in utter gloom even at 400 feet, at which height we were flying with the fog immediately above us. Luckily the country was well known to us. It would indeed have been courting disaster to have sent out men without an equally good knowledge.

Before leaving the ground, we had determined to commence the reconnaissance at the junction of the. opposing lines of trenches with the Lys Canal. This point was situated 1,000 yards from the south-eastern edge of the Forest of Nieppe. From there we could follow the line in a northerly direction, until, after flying over about 8 miles of country, we reached Meteren. As D—— had all his energies engaged in flying the machine, I signalled from time to time, by means of an outstretched arm, the direction I wished him to take. Reconnaissance, is, of course, the observer's "show."

Arriving at the canal, we crossed the trenches and flew parallel with them about 500 yards to the east. On reaching the large road leading to Merville, we followed it for a mile, returning the way we had come. This was done in the case of all roads of importance, with the object of missing no movement of troops. We had hoped that we might be able to justify our existence by taking back information of importance concerning an imminent attack. In this we were unfortunate. We had to console ourselves with the thought that, our negative information being thoroughly reliable, the powers that be could set their minds temporarily at rest concerning this part of the front.

Having reconnoitred the country around Vieux Berquin, Ouster-steene and Merris, we were entering upon our last stage, when ahead of us appeared a dense white wall. I had just time to shout out the one word "snow," and we were into it. Absolutely nothing could be seen but streaks of white fleeting past, which lashed unmercifully at exposed parts of the face. For how far the storm extended we could only surmise; in the meantime, D—— set a course for the north.

Luckily, in a couple of minutes we had passed through the snow and emerged into clearer air, where we climbed to a thousand feet. When to the east of the Trappist Monastery of Mont des Cats we turned about and made once more for Meteren. This little village had been taken by the Bosche three days before. We found the French lining trenches north-west of it; and, flying over the road as far as Bailleul, found no sign of enemy movement.

Our mission being definitely achieved, we returned to the aerodrome, where D—— made a perfect landing in spite of the tempestuous conditions. Our negative report was immediately 'phoned for the information of Brass Hats, and we repaired to the welcome warmth of a cheery mess and eloquent bar.

★★★★★★★★★★★★★★★★

One morning in early May I was awakened about four o'clock by very heavy gunfire. At once it occurred to me that either ourselves or the Bosche contemplated an attack, and this was the preliminary bombardment. Sometime afterwards our squadron recording officer entered waving a telephone message which stated that the Germans were attacking, and that a machine was to be sent off at once to reconnoitre the line. D—— and I had been detailed for the job. On looking out we found clouds lying so low that we realised that, unless a change for the better soon took place, our chances of bringing back information were extremely remote. We dressed at once, donned our flying kit, hastily drank a steaming cup of tea and clambered into our machine.

Our range of vision was bounded by a circle having as a radius 150 yards at the most. Our only hope lay in climbing through the clouds, and trusting that "hot air" patches would appear, through which we could look down on the country to be reconnoitred.

D—— took off, and, rapidly climbing, we entered the clouds and disappeared from view of those on the ground. Not until then did they realise the extreme "dudness" of the weather; and, anticipating our immediate return, orders were given for Very lights to be fired to guide us to the landing ground. To their surprise we did not return. The layer of clouds turned out to be of no great depth, and in a few seconds, we merged into daylight above them.

As we flew towards the lines—a fifteen minutes' flight—gaps here and there kept us informed as to our direction. On the other hand, there was no indication that the arrival of the sun would clear up the situation. Dark, forbidding clouds some thousands of feet above made such an event extremely unlikely. On approaching Nieppe Forest, which borders on the lines, we conferred together as to the advisability of going on, and decided to "carry on" for a time and hope for the best. The line to be reconnoitred stretched from the south-east edge of the Forest of Nieppe to Houthoulst Forest—a distance of about 40 miles, on any part of which the attack might be taking place.

We could not hope to see the whole of this; but, with great good luck, it was just possible that a hole in the clouds might coincide with the spot where the Bosche held his troops in readiness to advance. As for diving through the clouds, we were now flying just above them at

61

1,000 feet, and the idea of blindly charging into a tree or building did not appeal to us.

As we approached the lines west of Merville not a gap was to be seen. As far as eye could reach stretched a panorama of dull white cloud-country, in which mountains and *kopjes*, forests and gardens, plains and valleys, precipices and chasms were mingled together in riotous profusion. There was, today, little time to spare to ecstasise on the ever-varying beauties of cloudland. Our combined wits were required to get us back in safety to the aerodrome, for by now it was obvious that we must abandon our mission.

Turning away from Hunland, D—— steered by compass towards the north-west, hoping in about five minutes to strike Hazebrouck. No gap appeared until we were past that town, when we were given a few seconds in which to pick out from three railway lines the one leading to St. Omer, to the west of which our aerodrome lay.

A few minutes later, we caught a glimpse of the Cassel St. Omer road; and shortly afterwards we picked up Clairmarais Aerodrome, and finally St. Omer itself. Here, however, our troubles commenced; for the clouds became obstinately obdurate, and for ten minutes we flew above them without seeing a patch of mother earth.

Our aerodrome was six miles away, and we knew that by flying due west we should pass over it, or its vicinity. After five minutes D—— turned east again, and proceeded until he calculated he should be over St. Omer once more. It was evident that to get home we must dive through the clouds and take our chance of a collision. Navigation would be simple did not wind enter into the question. When we had started off there was little or, none; but it was evident, from the movements of the clouds, that this was not now the case. There was, therefore, the fear of drifting hopelessly off our course. We conferred, and came to the conclusion that we would dive down when east of the town.

A few seconds later for a very few moments a gap appeared; we both peered down, and at once recognised a landmark. It was a chalk pit, and had been already—before we knew the country well—of use in guiding us home. D—— made for the gap, hoping to make his way through before it closed up, but was too late. Knowing, however, that meadows and fields somewhat more low-lying than the bulk of the countryside were situated to its left front, he continued on; and our troubles were at an end when we pulled out in safety 70 feet above a farmhouse.

This incident may appear to contain only a slight element of danger, yet I must confess that I never have been so relieved as when it was over. The nerve strain was intense. It was the sort of experience which makes one feel ten years older. In our case we knew the country well. On such a day it would have been sheer idiocy to have sent up men that did net.

I am now more than ever convinced of the—for an airman to possess what is known as "An eye for country."

CHAPTER 7

Photographic Shows

Technically and officially known as a "Fighter Reconnaissance Squadron" our reputation will live, in the annals of the R.A.F. in the Great War, as a highly successful—perhaps the most successful—fighting unit. Our object in life was to get Huns. All our energies were focussed on that one aim; nothing else mattered very much. Yet we had side shows which we performed—without enthusiasm, but to the best of our ability. Amongst these were reconnaissances. Every offensive patrol was, to the observer, an opportunity for bringing back information for the benefit of the Intelligence Department.

I have known of one keen observer who appears to have been shot dead by a surprise attack when in the act of entering on a card an observation relating to a train—"Menin-Roulers—12.35." Such "accidents" occur; but, in the main, once an observer has gained a modicum of experience, he should have no difficulty in combining the search for Huns with that for movement.

In addition, we were at times engaged on Low Reconnaissances, types of which an attempt was made to describe in the last chapter. Infrequently, single machines were sent on special missions to spy out the land. Another pastime was the dropping of 112 lb. bombs on a selected target whenever we crossed the lines in formation. As our machines were not fitted with bomb-sights shooting was, to use a mild term, somewhat erratic. If a scrap was imminent the "egg" was at once disgorged—of course on the Hun side; the enemy never engaged us on ours.

For days—even weeks—Armentiéres station was our objective— but, so far as we were concerned, the safest place in the town was that same station. After some hundreds of bombs had been dropped (officially) on this target, a photograph revealed nothing more startling than a train with steam up. Wervicq was another place that was handed to us for treatment. A huge dump in due course went up in Comines, 2,000 yards away, so our efforts were not altogether in vain.

The moral effect of bombs falling in unexpected places, apparently from nowhere, must have been prodigious. Certainly, a percentage left a large gaping hole in fields—but there were others.

Another branch that at times demanded our temporary attention was photography. Whilst the Corps Squadrons with less handy machines took the enemy trench system and a mile or two beyond, we brought home "photees" of the country further afield. This was usually done in conjunction with our normal Offensive Patrols. The leading machine—and, perhaps, another—would have a camera fitted on board, adjacent to the observer; and, in the absence of Huns, the automatic process of supplying indisputable information would go on until the supply of plates, varying from thirty-six to seventy-two, was exhausted. As each plate accounted for a lump of territory 2 miles by 3 in extent, it was not long before "Intelligence" were fully supplied. On rare occasions photographs of a certain area would be urgently needed. Then a machine, perhaps with an escort, would be sent off posthaste.

In this chapter it is my intention to give an account of two photographic "shows" on which I was employed. There will be found nothing other than the *ordinaire* in the two outings. They will merely give an idea of the cut-and-dried manner in which photographs are taken on active service.

Whilst on the subject of photography, I propose to say a few words with the object of educating the lay public to a fuller appreciation of the work done—not by the fighting machines, but by those who actually do the work for which the Air Force in the field exists.

The public looks upon an airman as a getter, or prospective getter, of Huns. They would be surprised to learn how many pilots have never fired at an enemy aeroplane. It is not the job of all of them. Whilst there are squadrons who live to "crash" or be "crashed," there are others who concentrate on getting information, and signalling to the gunners where their shells fall. In fact, speaking roughly, the R.A.F. (excluding the bombers) is divided into two divisions—one that does the work, the other that enables it to be done.

The latter consists of the scouts and two-seater fighters, that patrol regularly to the German side of the line, and invariably further afield than the area in which the former operates. The object of the fighters is to prevent the Bosche obtaining information by shooting down

Three squadrons of "Bristol" Fighters paraded for inspection by General Sir William Robertson, at Spiel, Cologne

all and sundry who come towards our lines with that idea, and at the same time to protect our own machines by taking the offensive against enemy fighting machines in the sky. The further over we go to seek out the Germans, the greater the immunity enjoyed by our working machines.

In the days of cavalry, the horsemen that could defeat those of the opposing side returned with information. It is slightly different now. In the air, one branch of the service fights, thereby enabling another to obtain intelligence whilst usually immune from attack.

These remarks have unwittingly led my thoughts towards that much disputed phrase—"Mastery of the air." How is it, and how can it ever be, possible for one side to be Masters of the Air—to be supreme? In the case of a navy, it can be done, as we know well; but in the illimitable air it is another matter. A single determined pilot on a good machine can fool any number of opponents. It will never be possible so to patrol a long line that machines, or formations of machines, cannot pass over, under, or to a flank of the police on their beat. The word "ascendancy" seems more applicable. We have now, and have had for some time, an "ascendancy" in the air.

In other words, we are "top dog"; but supreme—no. Nor is the ascendancy measured by the comparative number of British and German planes destroyed, but rather by the value of material supplied to the respective Intelligence Departments, and by the quality of destructive work done by the respective artilleries.

Revenons à nos moutons. One day in early May three machines were ordered to "stand by" for a photographic show. By ten o'clock the sun was shining brilliantly; and, there being practically no wind, the day was an ideal one for the purpose. Photography is the observer's show, and each of us carried seventy-two plates. The area required comprised a narrow strip bordered on the east by Warneton, Houthem, Zandvoorde and Nieuwe Kruiseecke, and on the west by Messines, Hollebeke and Gheluvelt.

There are two cameras in general use in the R.A.F. One that takes in minute detail a small area of about 1,000 square feet, and another that, whilst giving less detail, reveals the main points of interest over a much larger area. Today we were provided with the former. As luck would have it the three machines all returned to the aerodrome within an hour of taking off without having procured a single picture. We and another had engine trouble. The survivor made for the objective, but, seeing a single Hun two-seater browsing far below, thought it too good an opportunity to be missed, and dived upon it. On getting within range the pilot's gun jammed, and, at the same time, five Hun scouts appearing, he had perforce to retire to our side of the lines. The rear gun, which had been keeping the pursuers a respectable distance away, now went permanently out of action, and a return to the aerodrome was rendered imperative.

On returning, all machines were made serviceable with commendable promptitude. It was now settled that only ours was to carry a camera, whilst the other two would act as escort. Owing to a misunderstanding we did the job alone. D——'s instructions were to climb to 4,000 feet to test his engine; and, if it was found to be O.K., we were to fire a *red* light as a signal to the others to join us. We bungled matters—misunderstood our instructions—fired no light—and, as there was no sign of movement on the aerodrome, decided to go without our escort. Climbing steadily, we crossed the lines at 17,000 feet in the neighbourhood of Warneton. For seventy-two plates to take the whole area was quite out of the question. It was better to concentrate on points of interest, and this we settled on doing. We decided on taking Warneton, Houthem, Zandvoorde and Gheluvelt.

At 17,000 feet a single machine may at times cross the lines unobserved by Archie. We did so now; and it was not until I had taken a dozen pictures of Warneton that the gunners woke to our presence. By the time they had made calculations as to our altitude I had finished the box of plates allotted to this area, and we were on the way to Houthem, three miles north. Here—possibly because no anti-aircraft battery was available—we were not worried, but allowed to concentrate all our energies not required in searching for Huns on the work in hand.

On arrival over Zandvoorde it was at once manifest that we were not to be allowed a walk-over. A battery of guns started as we approached the remnants of the village; by the time we had commenced operations they had the range to a nicety. D—— was flying in circles, and we trusted that what one plate missed another would obtain. *Wouff-wouff-wouff-wouff*—the shooting was too good for me. I suspended operations and conferred with D——. As a result of our deliberations, he dived down 1,000 feet, and then commenced to circle in the opposite direction. This ruse worked well. By the time, the Bosche had once more got our range we had successfully accounted for another batch of plates, and were making for our last objective, Gheluvelt.

Here we had a "cushy" job. The sky was full of machines, all of them British—Camels, S.E.'s and Dolphins. The majority were far below us and monopolized the attention of Archie to our utter exclusion. The show had been a successful one—provided no unforeseen disaster had occurred in connection with the camera. Luckily this was not the case, and results were entirely satisfactory.

Some days later we were again on a photographic "show," but, under quite different conditions. An Offensive Patrol was detailed from 5 to 6.30, and as "Intelligence" needed photographs of certain railways it was decided that it would traverse the country required, and, in the absence of Hun aircraft, take the "pictures."

The leader's machine was fitted with a camera, and also ours—not the type used on the last expedition, but one which took in very much more ground, approximately 2 by 3 miles at 16,000 feet.

The lines to be taken were Roulers to Courtrai and Roulers to Thourout. As the leader was likely to take the former, we decided that, provided the skies appeared clear, we would leave the formation over Roulers and fly to Thourout, taking photos *en route*.

We arrived over Roulers without incident, and watched the formation head south-east, with the leader flying directly above the railway line. We then turned towards the north and commenced operations. Photography, like other things, is simple—absurdly simple—after some experience. The pilot must fly straight, must not vary in speed and must keep always at the same altitude. If those points are attended to, the observer, who sits behind and works the instrument, has a sinecure. He has—or should have—a table beside him, showing the number of seconds of interval required between exposures at any given height and speed.

The wind is a factor which often upsets all calculations. At great heights there is always a breeze of greater or less velocity, and there is no instrument on the machine by which it can be gauged. Much experience is required before one can judge approximately the number of miles per hour that a machine is being assisted or retarded. It is advisable to study the meteorological reports before setting out, and to decide from them what conditions are likely to be met with, and plan accordingly.

Today at 16,000 feet there was, I had estimated, a wind of 30 miles per hour coming from the west. We wanted to make due north. To keep directly over our course, it was necessary to keep the nose of the machine inclining slightly westwards, in order to counteract the wind which otherwise would inevitably cause us to drift.

We had come to the conclusion that we should be delayed 10 miles per hour; therefore, when recording 80 on the speedometer we were actually covering the ground at a rate of 70 miles per hour. At that speed at 16,000 feet an exposure every seventy-five seconds had always given good results. Having settled on these details we could only pray that our calculations were moderately correct, and that the wind would not increase in volume.

When over the centre of the town I pressed the lever, thereby exposing the first of eighteen plates; I then operated the loading handle, pushing it backwards and forwards, which caused the exposed plate to be shunted into an empty box, and a fresh one to be brought into position. One exposure had to be made every minute and a quarter. Roughly the distance is 9 miles from Roulers to Thourout, including the towns themselves. Thus, seven exposures in all were required. Archie did not worry us, nor were any Huns observed; our plans worked out smoothly, and D—— kept directly over the line at 16,000 feet, his pilot showing 80 m.p.h.

Our job being accomplished we returned home without mishap or adventure and handed in the plates. They turned out all that could be desired; and when pasted together it was easy for the expert to pick out sidings, dumps, aerodromes, hospitals, etc., that had been established, extended or reduced since the last time photos had been taken of this section of the German railway system.

Today I wished that it were possible for me to put into words the extraordinary beauty of the scene. It was a perfectly clear day. Above stretched the familiar blue of the heavens, superb in their grandeur, solitary in their state, unsullied by cloud, smoke or human disfigurement. Below was the countryside spread out in panoramic outlines. Brought near, invitingly close at hand by the good visibility, reposed—

This royal throne of Kings,
This sceptred Isle,
This earth of majesty,
This seat of Mars—

—our "Island Home"—the Heart of the Empire. The dull prosaic outlines of the south and southeast coast were relieved from monotony by the white cliffs of Dover.

The sea reposed, calm and placid, decked with dainty vessels that, despite their peaceful demeanour, we knew to be keenly alive to the hazards of war. An airship, with an air of utter detachment, pursued its leisurely course. But that which changed the scene from an everyday one to one of indescribable beauty, was the pathway of purest gold which, many miles in width, was spread out from English to French shore. Those who have beheld the track of the sun from ocean liners or from coastal cliffs can form some idea of the supreme scene as viewed from miles above.

To gaze and meditate even when in contact with the everyday world, whether from *terra firma* or from the decks of ships, is a joy permitted to all who can purchase leisure—that most priceless possession. Their thoughts at such times are sacred. They almost leave their earthly surroundings and for a time are intellectually amongst the gods. But, when far aloft, breathing the purest air, in contact with little that savours of earthly disabilities, one can forget completely all of pettiness and sordidness that far below is wont to intrude upon our minds' outlook.

Few attempts up to the present have been made to describe the gorgeous, dazzling scenery, which is in itself a great reward reserved for those who explore the upper regions. Of all English poets of the past I wish that Byron could be with us now. He would have revelled in the new sensations and fresh experiences to be met with when flying. Our latter-day poets apparently await a state of tolerable comfort and safety before they will exert themselves to view the finest material for the muse yet supplied by the gods.

The majority of airmen see only the prose of flying and miss the poetry of it. But there are others to whom every flight in the air of heaven is an inspiration. To soar birdlike 20,000 feet towards the heavens; to see the whole world and the glory of it; to look down upon towns and villages, lakes and rivers, spread out in panoramic beauty leagues below; to view the fairest countryside divested of its sordidness, poverty and vice, and to see only its beauty; to feel oneself detached from all that makes life loathsome and repugnant; to breathe the purest air, and feel the sense of elation that comes from great heights; to refine the sense of solitude almost to pain; to adventure in spaces unknown to the mighty dead who perchance applaud from their Olympian heights; to dream unmolested of the future and forget the wretchedness of the present; to find purity at last; to gaze earthwards towards cathedrals and churches, and feel that all is not in vain; to feel those vague promptings that shall in future days of Peace inspire those who shall write of these glories—is to be of those who substitute for the dull days of Prose the throbbing emotional hours of Poetry.

CHAPTER 8

A Close Call

It happened on a gorgeous day in late June. The month had been one of the most perfect flying weather—pilots and observers had had a strenuous time. "Dud" days had been so few and far between that we had all 80 to 100 hours of war flying to enter into our log-books by the time the month had spent itself.

The squadron had once more definitely settled down to its regular routine of two or more offensive patrols each day. In the previous month we had created a record for the number of Huns crashed by a single squadron in any given month. Still possessing the nucleus of the experienced personnel who had been responsible for this, it is hardly necessary to state that our "tails were well up."

Yet as we flew towards the battleground of the skies on this superbly glorious morning it was no easy matter to detach our thoughts from scenes of Peace, and concentrate them on the anticipation of stern, relentless aerial warfare.

As we ascended higher and still higher into the: air of heaven the horizon rose to meet us. Moment by moment our range of vision extended. At first was visible a comparatively small area of the fair land of France! Then villages, towns, forests and rivers rose up to greet us. Soon much of martyred Belgium was incorporated in the landscape. Still higher, and the bays, harbours, ports and fishing villages of the coast came within view, followed by shipping on the seas and the indentations and white cliffs of the English coast. Spanning the waters, the golden bridge of the sun rested tranquilly.

The clear blue of the sky, the calm placidity of the waters, the apparent peacefulness of the countryside, filled one with a feeling of utter detachment. The keen pure air, exhilarating and inspiriting, banished petty cares and sordid imaginings,

It was sufficient to feast one's soul upon the outstretched panorama which poets shall one day sing and artists paint. In those future days of universal flight, one hopes it may be possible for the poorest of earth's dwellers to drink in the wonders of our old world as seen from above, and of our newly conquered ethereal empire. To describe the ever-changing glories that await the onrush of progress is possible only to the genius. He may be able to explain how men are affected in the same way as is the lark which, quitting the earth, sings the more joyously the higher she ascends, and on arrival on earth again grows quiet and pensive.

★★★★★★★★★★★★★★★★

A formation of scouts approaching from the east roused me from my reverie. They were, needless to say, British. Huns are not encountered on our side of the line. They turned out to be Dolphins—our latest and best machine when in the hands of good pilots. On looking round, I found that we were two miles to the north of Hazebrouck. The area over which we were in the habit of flying was all distinctly discernible. To the west its leading features included Dixmude, Ypres, Bailleul and Merville. Eastwards our range of offensive action was bounded by Thourout, Roulers, Inglemunster, Courtrai, Tourcoing, Roubaix, and Lille.

Ten miles from the latter lay Armentiéres, which, as a result of persistent bombing, was a hot-bed of anti-aircraft devilries. Each of our machines carried a 112 lb. bomb for delivery on the station of this important distributing centre. As we had no bomb-sights our missiles—as has been explained before—seldom hit their objective; but the uncertainty as to where they would fall cannot fail to have instilled the fear of God into the dwellers over a large area. The lines had been crossed south of Dickebusch Lake, and we had passed over Kemmel Hill—reduced by incessant shelling to the semblance of a huge sand heap. Thence the leader made for Armentiéres where Archie gunners were doubtless on the *qui vive* for their favourite target—a strong formation of "fat" two-seaters.

To reach the station it was necessary to fly over the town, and we were not left long in doubt as to the nature of our reception. In a few moments our machines were in a vortex of swirling black puffs which, accompanied by hectic "*wouffs,*" arrayed themselves in front and behind, above and below them. The barrage was really good, both in quantity and quality, but to be turned back by Archie is an unknown occurrence. Besides, he should not be taken too seriously. He is one of the petty worries of life which, whilst doing little damage, is apt to annoy by incessant repetition.

Our formation was, in spite of Archie's hostility, well bunched together—an undeniable proof of good morale—and turning some way west of the station so as to fly parallel with the rails the leader led us over it. A few seconds later twelve bombs were speeding earthwards and doing their "bit" towards winning the war.

For some time, a number of black specks had been visible apparently circling round above Lille. Probably they were gaining height with the ultimate object of scrapping us. When at about the same height as the centre of our formation of twelve, they flew leisurely towards us. There were ten of them, and the half-hearted manner in which they approached gave the undeniable impression that the pilots were not keen on a fight. As was humorously remarked in the subsequent mess postmortem, a Big Brass Hat in the German Flying Corps had in all probability despatched them on their mission while he watched events from a coign of vantage.

As they came nearer it was seen that the formation was composed of Pfalz Scouts and Fokker Biplanes. The latter had only recently made their bow before the British Air Force, and were considered superior to anything the enemy had in the skies.

Following the leader our formation had been steadily climbing, with the result that by the time the clash came our machines one and all had the advantage in height. As we had the sun behind us, it is just possible that we were unobserved until, on a red light being fired from the leader's machine, we dived upon them. They immediately put their noses down and dived under our formation, when they zoomed up again. Had they made for Hunland matters would have been simplified for us—we could have continued our dive. As it was, our machines had to be pulled out preparatory to diving again. The result was that—as so often occurs when the first attack is not successful—a dogfight ensued.

My Pilot (D—— had gone on leave to England), one of the best the squadron possessed, fired a few rounds when his gun hopelessly jammed. A moment afterwards a black-crossed camouflaged bird flitted by underneath our machine and only about 50 yards away. She was almost in a blind spot, *i.e,*. in a position in which I could not bring my gun to bear upon her. Only by placing it in an almost vertical position and standing on the seat was I able to get off a few rounds. Results, as might have been expected, were not apparent. Almost immediately afterwards another Hun flew by 100 yards to the right and below me.

This was a comparatively easy shot; I sighted and pulled the trigger. Three rounds rewarded my efforts. Cursing volubly, I examined the gun and found that the striker had broken. Of this we do not carry a spare part, and my gun was therefore useless. Our machine was now in the general *mêlée* without a single serviceable weapon.

The pilot conferred with me and we came to the conclusion that we had better make our way back over the lines. Possibly it would have been better policy to have climbed well above the fight and to have "sat" there until the Huns were defeated and chased away. We could then have placed ourselves in the centre of the formation and, when near the lines, could have separated from the remainder and crossed without fear of molestation. As it was, we had over 10 miles to fly over enemy country without any means of defence—an adventure that I would not again enter upon lightly, as may be gathered from subsequent events. We were about 3 miles south-east of Armentiéres when we started to make for home. The pilot headed for the nearest part of the line, which was slightly east of Bailleul. Luckily, we were helped by the wind, which increased our speed by 20 or more miles per hour.

All went well for a couple of minutes. No enemy aircraft were to be seen. But we had not reckoned upon the grim tenacity displayed by Archie, when on a clear day he spots what he takes to be a "lame duck" retiring from a fight. We were flying at 12,000 feet—a range at which he is astonishingly proficient. There is nothing he revels in so much as concentrating on a single machine. Never, however, in my wildest dreams had I imagined that he was capable of such impassioned, envenomed "Hate" as he now displayed. From the moment we came within range of Armentiéres batteries until enemy scouts relieved him of responsibility a mile from the lines, he haunted us mercilessly.

Our course lay, unfortunately, adjacent to Steenwercke, the home of more than 'usually expert gunners; but those of Bailleul also were by no means to be despised. "*Wouff-Wouff-Krunch-Krunch*" barked high explosives on all sides. *Hiss-s-s-s-s* shrieked the flying fragments. Side-slipping, changing direction, climbing, diving—all were of no avail. To dodge one swarm was to rush headlong into another. Yet the machine was as serviceable as ever. With the exception of a few holes in the wings and fuselage the Hun had accomplished nothing for his vast expenditure of material and energy.

Six miles of the journey had been covered. Behind us trailed back

"BRISTOL" FIGHTERS STRAFING A HUN AERODROME

puffs, at first clearly defined, and at last so intermingled that our course could be compared to that of an ocean liner leaving a drifting smudge to mark its progress. When near Steenwercke I experienced the fright of my life. The tail was suddenly shot up into the air and the machine dropped like a stone for 200 or more feet through the smoke of the exploded shell. Strange to relate, we were not touched by the flying fragments. Shortly afterwards there was a loud vociferous *krunch* most alarmingly near. Looking round I saw that a wire had snapped—luckily it was not a flying wire.'

Almost at the same moment the engine stopped, having been switched off by the pilot. As we found out on landing, a piece of metal had cut through the exhaust pipe and the front petrol tank. It was extremely lucky that we did not go down in flames. On being deluged with petrol the pilot let go of everything in the machine and, using two hands, opened the radiator vane. Then he switched off the engine, cut off the petrol, and pulled back the throttle. After giving the petrol in the front tank time to escape, he switched the engine on again.

By this time, we were approaching Bailleul. Archie had given us no respite. Through efforts to dodge him and the engine having been switched off for a time we had lost height and were now at 6,000 feet. Needless to say, Archie had not diverted me from searching the skies diligently for enemy machines. In our present plight we should have been the coldest of "cold meat" to even the most useless pilot in the German Flying Corps. On the other hand, an attack by hostile 'planes would bring with it relief from Archie's incessant din.

This is precisely what did happen. Three specks had been growing larger for some minutes, diving in our direction from enemy country. I had hoped they were British machines, but as they came nearer it was plainly evident that they were Pfalz Scouts. This tends to show that whilst it is one thing to have an *ascendancy* in the air, it is quite another to be *supreme*. No matter how great an ascendancy we possess, we can never hope to maintain in the air a sufficiency of machines to ensure that roving German pilots keep to any given boundary line. In fairness, however, it must be admitted that to fly 10 miles over Hunland and sight Huns and no Allied 'planes is in the nature of a unique experience.

When about 2,000 feet above us two of the scouts pulled out of their dive and sat up above, whilst their companion continued towards us. He did not appear over-confident. Had he taken his courage in both hands and come straight for us I should in all probability not be alive to tell the tale. Within shooting range, the fact that we were without a serviceable rear gun would have been self-evident.

Whatever may have been his ideas on the subject, he was content to flatten out 300 to 500 yards to our rear and slightly above. At this rather hopeless range he commenced to fire. Not a single bullet found its mark. As he appeared to be gaining confidence and to be creeping nearer it occurred to me that my Very pistol might be of some utility. Loading it with a red light, I fired it up into the air. This was followed in quick succession by three others. The Hun turned and climbed towards his companions. The pilot, having been a witness of our ignominious "strafing" by Archie, can hardly have thought that we were acting as bait. It is likely that he interpreted the lights as a call for assistance to British machines which we had seen and he had not. In any case it was a vastly humorous incident.

A few more moments and we were over the trenches. My pilot flew at a low altitude and with extreme care, being apprehensive lest a fire should break out, but arrived at the Aerodrome without further incident. Landing is unfortunately a corollary to all flights. I was by no means sure that wheels or undercarriage had not been damaged by Archie. Such an event would make landing a dangerous proceeding at all times—just now, however, it was the one thing to be avoided owing to the probability of fire. There was no need for pessimism however. A perfect landing was made and our troubles were over.

CHAPTER 9

A Very Black Day

It is with great satisfaction that one sees a German machine go down in flames. This appears to imply a degree of callousness of which in normal times one would have little cause to be proud when it is remembered that a fellow-creature and a brave man has died a ghastly death. In extenuation, however, it must be pointed out that the average airman, seeing so little of the occupant, and so much of the machine, gives—at any rate during a scrap—all his thoughts to downing the latter whilst completely ignoring the human element.

It is quite another matter when one of our own 'planes comes to such an untimely end. In the case of a two-seater, it means that not one but two pals have gone, that two familiar faces will be tonight missing from the mess. They are apparently soon forgotten and their successors are jolly good fellows. But it is some time before the spectacle of the burning machine bids a final *adieu* to one's dreams.

During some months' war flying I saw several of the enemy's but only one of our machines shot down in flames. Sometimes the conflagration progresses slowly—doubtless maddeningly so to the luckless victims—occasionally a landing is made. More often the catastrophe is a painfully protracted form of hell.

On the occasion to which I am now referring our men, I am sure, did not suffer at all, but death was immediate. The patrol on which it occurred was a more than usually interesting and exciting one; and so, the incident—trivial in a sense in war days—will be described in its proper sequence.

It was midsummer. For some days it had been hot, sultry and oppressive. Flying—even to one used to the Tropics—was a relief from the close atmosphere which prevailed in and around our Armstrong huts and iron-roofed mess. Fortunately, cool mornings and evenings made up for much of the day's discomfort.

The "show" was an early morning one. We were to be on our beat protecting from molestation the artillery and reconnaissance machines from 6 to 7.30. D—— and I were called at half-past four, got into our flying kit, swallowed a *soupçon* of breakfast preliminary to a more complete meal contemplated on our return, and went to the Squadron office for the *powwow*. At this the major told us the objective on which bombs were to be dropped; Ghelewe on the main road from Menin to Ypres had been selected. This was the first time we had been ordered to pay attention to this little hamlet, which from the air appears to be so thoroughly peaceful and happy.

Surrounded by meadows, fields and tiny farm-buildings, and with its unpretentious church in the centre of a few score humble dwellings, it is a typical Flanders village. One cannot but regret the destruction inevitable in war, and I felt sorry that it was my duty to do my best to lay waste this picturesque hamlet, thereby instilling terror into the hearts not only of German troops, but of Belgian women and children, still living in their loved homes at the mercy of their conquerors.

We set off at a quarter past five, and were soon heading towards the east. The sun had not yet made its appearance; but, outlined against the pale blue of the night, all the colours of the rainbow heralded his approach. In the west the full moon looked on calmly, unconcernedly, preparatory to handing over the duties of illuminating the war zone to its more brilliant rival. Before we reached the lines the sun had risen—a huge, flaming sheet of dazzling light. Sunrise as seen from the air is a gorgeous sight. Piercing, dazzling rays penetrate into the valleys dispersing the mists, and crown the hilltops with haloes of gold. There will assuredly come a time when artists will vie with one another in painting the scene.

It is in the early mornings that one may hope to hide most effectually in the sun. Then, mingling with the low-lying mists, it provides a background against which one can fly with every prospect of being unobserved. The Germans, of course, are adepts in taking advantage of this. A very keen look-out was necessary to guard against surprise.

We passed over the ruins of Ypres, amongst which one now looked in vain for noble edifices. Then, steering south-east, in a couple of minutes we reached the spot where Gheluvelt once stood, and which marked the fringe of this shell-ploughed belt of once fertile soil. From here traces of war became less frequent, and the road could be followed towards our objective—a short distance off.

Successful bomb-dropping is not so simple as is generally believed. If it were only necessary to release one's missile when immediately above the target the material damage inflicted would be infinitely greater than is generally the case. To find its mark, however, a bomb must be released before the target is reached. The distance in front varies with the height and speed of the machine, the weight and shape of the bomb and the direction and velocity of the wind—to mention only the most important factors. As a result of improved sights, aided materially by the increased experience of pilots and observers, fair shooting is now, I understand, being done by our regular bombing squadrons; but the margin of error is still great.

Our machines were not fitted with sights. This, added to the fact that "bombing" was for us a "side show" in which we had received no special instruction, did not tend towards precision in aim. Nevertheless, a village, however small, is a comparatively large target, and at least we could count upon some moral effect.

We relied upon experience rather than upon the methodical working out of tables—which, indeed, in the absence of sights are of small value. Flying, as we usually did, at between 12,000 and 18,000 feet we had to release our bombs some thousands of feet before reaching the target. Today we did useful work, for the nine "eggs"—one from each machine—were seen to burst in the village, where it is hoped damage was inflicted on German war material and personnel in addition to morale.

Being now free to give our undivided attention to Huns in the air the leader turned north, and we flew, as we had done many times before, parallel with the Menin-Roulers road.

Five enemy machines had ere this been sighted coming from the north-east. When they first came into view four were flying in perfect diamond formation, with the remaining machine a short distance away to the right. It occurred to me that the latter was piloted by an instructor, who was giving a lesson in formation flying. This supposition was supported by the fact that on coming nearer to us he placed himself slightly in advance—the four forming a line behind him. No attempt was made at concealment; but, having the advantage in height, on arriving within reasonable distance they dived on us, firing the while. They did not continue their dive to point-blank range. It is doubtful if the most daring came within 100 yards. But after firing much ammunition without inflicting any noticeable damage they dived below us.

In the light of what transpired a few moments afterwards there is little doubt that this was one of the few occasions when the Huns employed a ruse in the hope of accounting for some of our machines. We did not know it, but six more enemy 'planes were "sitting" serenely in the sun, waiting for us to become seriously involved with the five below. We were a formation of nine machines, and it was not the business of any one to deliberately watch the skies for enemy reinforcements from above. The formation leader nominally sees to this, and having had experience of the sun, both in offence and defence, he would have been perhaps more usefully employed if, instead of speeding to increase his bag of Huns, he had left the fighting to the remainder and kept his eyes open for developments.

Be that as it may, we all concentrated on the destruction of the five attackers who had flattened out below us. In this we were successful, as D—— shot down one, and another fell to the gun of the flight commander. We had thus made short work of the "bait," for the remaining three had dived down lower than we were in the habit of going.

It was now the enemy's turn. We cannot expect to have it always our own way. As I afterwards heard, six machines suddenly appeared out of the sun, but of these I saw only three; whether the others attacked *en masse* a single machine or singled out each its own prospective victim, I have no idea. They, however, succeeded in sending one of our machines spinning earthwards. No one saw if it crashed or landed safely. All were too busy protecting their own machines to pay attention to anything else. In addition, they shot an observer, whose dead body was removed after the scrap at the nearest aerodrome. One of these three Huns was claimed by an observer who, whilst unable to watch her to the ground, was positive that he had sent her down out of control. It is of the other three that I can write with certainty. It was they who between them brought down one of ours in flames.

D—— was cruising around rather aimlessly—the first scrap being over—when, keeping my eyes towards the sun, I saw one of our two-seaters emerge out of it. She was flying straight, and diving on it were no less than three Fokker Biplanes. She headed in our direction. By the time she was within about 100 yards of us the Huns had gained ground and were shooting for all they were worth. Our pilot, a new one—it was his second show—appeared to have no better plan than to beat a retreat, leaving his observer to protect the rear—a somewhat difficult task for one gun against six; and as a matter of fact, it is likely that he was put out of action by the first burst of Hun fire, for whilst the Germans' tracer smoke was very apparent there was no indication that our man had his gun in action. It is possible, of course, that it had jammed for breakages became very dangerously frequent during the last year of the war.

Just as the red, white and blue circles of the British machine showed up distinctly, almost directly above us, the persistent shooting of the Huns had its expected effect. In a second the thing was done. At one moment a perfectly good two-seater fighting 'plane was a thing in being. The next a sheet of flame was in its stead. There was no warning—no small licking flame growing larger—but just a flash of fire enveloping with lightning speed the whole machine. For a moment the flame continued onwards. Then it inclined towards the earth and went headlong down, 20 to 30 feet to our right.

All this occurred in a few seconds. I had wasted no time in drawing D——'s attention and had swung my gun up in anticipation of accounting for one at least of the attackers. This should have been easy—absurdly easy. The enemy machines were almost directly above me and it was only necessary to put a barrage of bullets in front of any single one and await her interception with them. With this idea I singled out the leading machine and pulled the trigger. Just two rounds was the nett result. This was a bitter disappointment, for I had never had such a "sitting" target.

In the meantime, we were in imminent danger, for the Huns having accounted for one machine might reasonably be expected to pay attention to us. If they had, it is probable that they would have shot us down; for in the circumstances the absence of a serviceable rear gun was a very great handicap. An extractor had broken. This jamb takes an inconsiderable number of seconds to remedy, but there was no possibility of doing so before the Huns might be expected to attack. Luckily for us, however, they were apparently satisfied with what they had done, for, diving steeply, they were quickly clear of danger from us as were we, much to our relief, from them.

We had lost two machines, officially designated as "missing," and an observer. Of the enemy we had accounted for two crashed and another out of control, i.e., believed destroyed. Losses were therefore approximately equal. Yet it was for us a very black day indeed. We were not accustomed to losing more than one machine in any "scrap"—in fact, we seldom had casualties.

It must be remembered that the two "missing" pilots were new men, practically devoid of experience of war flying. It is so often that lives are lost in the learning stage—but this is only natural. Experience has to be bought; but the price in flying is heavy, and in many cases unredeemable.

And thou whose wounds are never healed,
Whose weary race is never won,
O, Cromwell's England! must thou yield
For every inch of ground, a son?

Chapter 10

Balloons and Balloonatics

Very little is known by the general public about balloons. Londoners have seen, during the last year or so, huge gas-bags some thousands of feet up in the air, and have been told that they are "sausages," or "kite" balloons. That they are used for watching the movements of the enemy they also vaguely realise; of their history, or of the nature of the work done by the observer who sits on a wicker basket below the huge inflated bag, they know little or nothing.

The first balloon to be employed in battle was used by the French at the Battle of Fleurus in 1794, when Colonel Coutelle is said to have supplied observations of the utmost importance to the General Commanding. Even greater service was the effect on the morale of the Austrians, who were discouraged by the Paani that the French knew all that they were doing, whilst they knew nothing of the enemy's movements. With their one balloon the French were supreme, in the air. Supremacy is, I am afraid, out of the question in these modern days of vast aerial fleets; but to know more of the enemy's movements than he knows of yours has always been the first *desideratum*, and is a sure stepping-stone to ultimate victory.

The gallant colonel had four hot-air balloons constructed and, his command was known as the Aerostatic Corps—the first Flying Corps to be formed. Napoleon used this novel method of obtaining information in Egypt, but appears to have been unfavourably impressed—for in about 1802 the school of the Aerostatic Corps was abolished.

The Russians and the French made efforts to employ balloons usefully during the years that followed; but it was not until 1849 that they were again used—this time by the Austrians. In 1856 they were employed by the Russians from Sebastopol; in 1859 by the French against the Italians; and in the American Civil War by the Federal Army.

Towards the end of 1914 the R.N.A.S. at Dunkirk, having seen the single German-built balloon of the Belgian Army, quickly got to work upon one. They were soon followed by the R.F.C. who, by the end of 1916, had several in operation. Later, thanks to Captain Cacquot of the French Airship Service, an efficient type was evolved.

Without going into details, it may be said that a balloon is a cylindrical chamber filled I with hydrogen, and is thus rendered lighter than air; attached to it—and of course below it—is a wicker basket, which will take two observers comfortably. The *raison d'être* of the latter is to supply information—not only of the movements of the enemy's troops, transport, and trains, but of anything likely to be of interest to Intelligence. Whilst they are at times—and especially on clear days—invaluable in this respect, it is in conjunction with the artillery that the bulk of their work is done.

Kite balloon observers must know their country so well that, on seeing a flash from any part of it revealing the presence of a hitherto unspotted German gun, they can without undue delay inform the gunners of the exact spot. If not otherwise employed, an affiliated battery is asked on the 'phone to. neutralise, *i.e.,* cause the hostile guns to cease fire.

During this operation the observer informs the gunners of the burst of shells, thus directing them on to the target; known targets are similarly engaged with the object of destroying them, the time for the "shoot," and other particulars, being arranged over the 'phone or in consultation the evening before.

There have been many discussions in R.A.F. messes as to the relative advantages of kite balloons and aeroplanes in spotting for the guns. Whilst it is claimed that a 'plane flying directly over the target can see to a nicety where the shells burst, on the other hand the rapidity of motion, annoyance from Archie, and the necessity for looking for Huns precludes the observation from being more than approximately accurate. Balloon observers it must be admitted on exceptionally clear days can put in—as they do—exceedingly good work. When they can see the target distinctly, they probably are of greater utility than the flying men; but unfortunately, there are so many days when hazy conditions cause them to be out of action. During the winter months especially, they are of little or no use.

"Balloonatics," as the observers call themselves, are generally considered to have a soft billet. It must be confessed that to the muddy warrior in the trenches their job appears an enviable one. They work only on fine days and so are always dry and comfortable. They live in luxury in *châteaux* or farmhouses miles behind the lines.

Yes—without a doubt they have a moderately "cushy" job. It must be remembered, however, that the majority of them are more or less "crocked." I knew one company, comprising two balloons, the entire personnel of which were officially unfit for service in the infantry.

But it would be a great mistake to suppose that ballooning is free from danger and nerve strain; whilst casualties are few, the effect on the nerves is such that a year's observing is enough for any ordinary man. There is always the fear of an attack by hostile aircraft. As often as not the observers themselves do not see the 'plane or 'planes attacking them, owing to the sky above them being hidden by the balloon. Perhaps the whirr of an engine or the *cac-cac-cac* of a machine-gun is the first intimation.

Now, however, that machine-gunners are constantly on the look-out—in addition to the Archie gunners—this seldom occurs, but warning is given on the 'phone if the necessity for a parachute descent appears likely. It is not pleasant to sit on the edge of a basket 4,000 feet in the air, waiting momentarily for the word "jump"—which may, or may not, come. If it does not the nerve strain has been intense. If it does a parachute descent is a thing that appeals to few; for although the parachute always does open, there is the ever-present thought—especially to the highly strung—that it may not.

The Huns have recently adopted the practice of shooting at the Observers as they descend—a fiendish thing to do in my opinion.

The actual descent is in its way an interesting experience, once the parachute has opened. Personally, I have only once made a descent, and it was not due to the enemy's action. I passed through countless years when, after jumping from the basket, I waited for the parachute to open. The actual time was only a matter of two or three seconds, but it seemed an eternity as I fell—fell—fell. Then suddenly there was an awning above me and all was quiet and peaceful. I appeared to be hardly moving. When the ground became moderately near it was surprising how quickly it rose up towards me. Then I realised that I was descending at a considerable rate, and I prepared for a bump on landing. Luckily, I struck moderately soft meadow land and was not even bruised. Also, there was no wind, so I was not dragged.

Many a leg has been broken through landing on hard materials, houses, roads, etc., whilst it is an unpleasant experience to get caught in a tree. A strong wind on the ground has often been the cause of observers being dragged some distance, causing them, especially in reconquered territory, to get severely cut by barbed wire or other debris.

Another nerve-racking ordeal to which the balloonatic has, perforce, to submit is hostile shelling. Usually, the enemy aims for the winch, which is mounted on a motor lorry, but at times he goes for the balloon itself. The occupants carry on to the best of their ability; but to watch shrapnel bursts approaching hearer and nearer is demoralising—to say the least.

Were it not for annoyance from the enemy, ballooning is an interesting job. On a clear day one can see for miles; and, once a thorough knowledge of the country has been obtained, it is astonishing how much useful information a really good observer can collect. The balloon being stationary he is at liberty to study suspicious objects at his leisure: with the aid of glasses, and his experience enables him to see through the enemy's attempts. at camouflage. What appears to be a group of poplars of mushroom growth cannot fail to be a concealed battery. Similarly, he will spot new trenches, roads, light railways, or any new feature. The "spotting" for the gunners is of more than ordinary interest, owing to the fact that the success of the "shoot" depends as much upon the observer as the gunner.

In an attack the occupants of a balloon, besides being able to do much useful work in keeping commanders informed of its progress, have a better all-round bird's-eye view of the battlefield than anyone. The fact that they can hear distinctly the roar of the guns and the crackle of musketry enables them to get a much better idea of the progress of a battle than the men in the planes, whose ears are deafened by their own engine.

At intervals our squadron acted as escort to a formation of scouts who had been told off to strafe balloons. Perhaps the most successful "War" of this kind in which we participated was in the early days of June, when a squadron of camels shot down three in flames.

The ordinary tracer bullet seldom causes a balloon to burn, and so a special bullet is employed. It is known as "soft-nosed-Buckingham" and is nearly always successful. This special ammunition is not used against enemy aeroplanes; and when taken up for use against balloons a card, signed by the general officer commanding the Royal Air Force in the field, is pinned to the cockpit of the user, certifying that it is for use against balloons only. There is no doubt as to the necessity for this. One of these bullets if lodged in one's person would, it is said, proceed to burn away all flesh and bone in its vicinity.

The usual height at which balloons fly is 3,000 to 4,000 feet. Our squadron seldom went down so low when employed on Offensive Patrols, and although some of us would amuse ourselves by firing a magazine at them from extreme range, it is probable that our chances of inflicting damage were infinitesimal. Therefore, we seldom bagged a "sausage"—only on a single occasion have I seen one destroyed by fire by our pilots and observers. That was during a "dogfight" with the enemy; when a pilot, having dived on a Hun and shot him down saw, on pulling out of his dive, a balloon 1,000 feet below him. He considered the opportunity too good to be missed; and making straight for it fired a hundred rounds of ordinary ammunition into the fabric without any apparent result. He then passed to the side of the target, and gave an opportunity to his observer, who carried on the good work to such effect that the balloon went down to earth in flames and smoke.

For some days before the particular balloon "strafe" which I am about to describe, weather had been extremely "dud"; and having been ordered to hold ourselves in readiness to escort a Scout Squadron in this interesting job, we 'longed for fine weather that the Hun might unsuspectingly put up his balloon line.

For four days we remained inactive. By the fifth, prospects had improved; and by twelve o'clock a message came through, informing the squadron commander that visibility over the lines was moderately good, and that "sausages" were up in their usual numbers behind the German lines.

It was arranged that we should meet the scouts over Cassel at 1.30. There were to be fifteen "strafers," and our escorting party was to be a strong formation of twelve machines. The hour appointed found us at the rendezvous, where we were shortly joined by the machines we were to escort. They were at 7,000 to 8,000 feet, and we climbed above them to heights ranging from 10,000 to 14,000. The object of our presence was to protect the "strafers" from attack from above, and generally to enable them to concentrate on the work in hand, secure in the knowledge that they were immune from surprise attacks. The Hun had about fifteen balloons between Merville and Ypres— stretched out at intervals of 3 to 4 miles behind their front line.

The plan was to make a bee line for the fifth balloon to the east of Merville, and when two miles from it for the attackers to split up into three parties. One of these would make for the gas-bags in the centre and the other two for the flanks. In the meantime we would hover above on guard, taking the while a lively interest in proceedings.

No enemy aeroplanes were in sight. The scouts, on a signal from their leader, split up and dived on various balloons. The Huns by this time had scented danger and had commenced to haul down. They were too late, however. The scouts were upon them—diving, zooming, and diving again—pouring into them lead and fire. The sight viewed from above was a thrilling one. Archie batteries from the ground below the balloons opened up a murderous fire, whilst, machine guns doubtless took their part in the defence.

Very soon each sausage as it descended was surrounded by puffs of smoke, in, out, and through which the tiny scouts twisted and turned. In one or two cases the fire was so hot and accurate that the defence succeeded in warning off attackers who had failed in their first onslaught. Observers were scurrying to the side like rats from a sinking ship. It is advisable to waste no time in jumping out when a plane on business bent appears. At one time I saw four parachutes descending slowly and calmly to earth; and I must confess to having a fellow feeling for the observers, and to hoping that they would land without mishap. This they probably did, as there was very little wind to cause them to be dragged on reaching the ground.

In less time than it has taken to write about it, the "strafe" was over and the scouts, having been in some cases successful and necessarily in the majority unsuccessful, formed up in rear of their leader. In spite of Archie's utmost efforts, they had suffered no casualties. No machine had been seriously damaged and no pilot had been wounded. |

The bag totalled three—a highly creditable performance, although pilots reported having fired hundreds of rounds without result, thus giving the impression that today, for some reason, it was more than usually difficult to cause the fabric to burn. Of the three two had been got in the first rush, within a few seconds of one another. There is nothing vastly spectacular in a balloon coming down in flames. One sees the whole bag suddenly transformed into a mass of flame which immediately commences to fall earthwards. In a moment or two dense black smoke takes the place of the flames and descends slowly, growing smaller in bulk the while.

The third victim had a stomach for incendiary bullets. Two 'planes expended many rounds upon it in the initial attack; and it was not until they had run the gauntlet of Archie and machine gun bullets for what seemed to them an uncomfortably long time, that it obliged them by doing the needful, after 500 or more rounds had been expended against it.

Chapter 11

Noteworthy Scraps

During the month of May our squadron had shot down seventy-five German machines. Of these fifty had been confirmed as having "crashed" and the remaining twenty-five had gone down "out of control." Our losses were three machines "missing" and two observers wounded.

Whether in retaliation for the severe strafing they had undergone, or with the object of bringing relief to Armentiéres—upon which we had for days been dropping bombs—is problematical, but one day in early June the German Flying Corps made a "dead set" at our squadron. The combination of vastly superior forces against our formation may have been purely accidental, but in my own mind I am convinced that a carefully thought-out plan was put into execution with the object of entrapping us.

It may be asked; how did the Huns know at what time your squadron might be expected over the lines? On a clear day—the whereabouts of our aerodrome being known to them—it is probable that from rising ground with a pair of field glasses they could see our machines shortly after taking off. By at once informing Squadron Offices by 'phone they could have machines in the sky awaiting us by the time we were likely to arrive. This was apparently the case today when, on crossing the lines, two of the enemy's formations could be seen, whilst a third was too far up in the skies to be visible. They all had the same object in view.

The first formation that came under my notice was north-east of Armentiéres. They were being badly Archied. The natural inference was that they were allied 'planes. Had we believed this, we would have flown towards our objective, serenely confident that Huns were conspicuous by their absence and that friendly machines were in the neighbourhood. Wise in our own conceits, we would have walked into the trap so skilfully prepared by the German Flying Corps staff.

"'Won't you walk into my parlour?' said the spider to the fly." Fortunately, the more experienced of us were not to be caught so easily. The shooting was bad—abnormally, unnaturally bad. Shells were bursting far below the machines, and black puffs were floating away thousands of feet to their right and left. "Dud Archie," I shouted to D——, who nodded his head in agreement. The machines were German. We had spotted the "camouflage" and were quite sure our leader—an old hand at the game—had done so too. He would now be more than ever on his guard, for it was evident that some pre-arranged plan was being unfolded.

Specks had by now become visible south-west of the town. As they grew larger it was noticed that a fight was in progress. Scouts were diving, zooming and circling round in the good old style. If our leader had not seen through the Archie trick, he would probably have led us at full speed to join in the fray. He was suspicious, however; and rightly surmised that this was another Hun ruse—so old as to have whiskers on it. Had he led us to the assistance of what he might have supposed to be British scouts, we would have been hopelessly involved. On the arrival the Huns—for they were all enemy planes—would have given up their stunting performance and attacked us. The Archied convoy would have joined in, and the sudden advent of forty to fifty more from far above would have placed us in an unenviable position from which few, if any, of our machines would have escaped.

We were not yet aware of the existence of the very formidable formation hovering over the town. For the moment the position was as follows: In front of us lay Armentiéres, on either side of which were eight or nine hostile—machines. There was nothing, so far, to cause one moment's uneasiness: a single British two-seater is a match for two German scouts. To the veriest tyro in aerial warfare, it was evident, however, that if our deductions were correct, the Huns had some scheme afoot as yet unfathomed by us. I kept an eye on the leader's machine that we might lose no time in backing him up. At the same time, I searched the skies for further developments in the form of enemy 'planes.

D—— was before me in spotting them. He pointed to the south, where after a few moments I barely distinguished several tiny specks, far up in the sky. We were at 13,000 feet, whilst they were at heights varying from 17,000 to 19,000 feet. After a few moments' concentration upon them I came to the conclusion that there must be at least forty hostile machines in this "circus."

Has the leader seen them? was the question that at once arose. There was no means of knowing. But if not, it was of vital importance that he should be informed. We were heading straight into the Hun's carefully arranged and well-timed trap. I shouted to D—— that we had better let them know. He agreed, and putting the nose of the machine down was soon flying abreast of the leading 'plane. I had intended to point with the spare joy sticks towards the specks, followed, if necessary, by Morse code signals.

There was, however, no need for this. The pilot had spotted them a few moments before, and as we came alongside was conferring with his observer. They apparently agreed that discretion was in this case the better part of valour, for the direction was changed from south-east to due west. That brave man and chivalrous fighter Baron von Richthofen has himself written, *"it is foolish to die unnecessarily a hero's death."*

Had we snapped our fingers at the Huns and their wily traps and given battle the remark, *"C'est magnifique, mais ce n'est pas la guerre,"* would have been indeed justified. It would have been a foolish thing to do. Many a good airman would be alive today had commonsense and prudence more often prevailed against stupid bravery and mad recklessness.

As we flew parallel with the trenches and about a mile over Hunland, the two formations from the neighbourhood of Armentiéres threw off their mask and proclaimed themselves in their true colours, joining forces and edging towards us. The large formation also came nearer, but still kept at a great height. For some months past German machines had given up venturing on, or near, our side of the lines; and although in such vastly superior numbers they appeared to be in no mood to do so now. Seventeen Pflaz Scouts hung on to our flanks, keeping at a convenient distance.

Their object was to lure us after them and, even at the eleventh hour, give the swarm of Fokker Biplanes above their opportunity for a sudden dive. We had no intention of obliging them. Artillery machines were flying up and down below us. It was consolatory to know that, although we had to retire from our bombing objective, we were still able to ensure safety for the working 'planes it was our duty to protect.

Shortly afterwards a large formation of S.E.'s came into view, heading in our direction from the vicinity of Cassel. The Huns now realised that their effort to destroy us had failed. They turned and made off over Hunland and in a few minutes were out of sight. They had at least the satisfaction of having prevented us from dropping our bombs on Armentiéres. As they had to be disposed of, other targets were selected, according to the fancy of individual pilots and observers. Steenwerck, Merris and Neuf Berquin were amongst the towns and villages that were reminded that we still held an ascendency in the air.

In spite of much that has been written on the subject by war correspondents and nonflying writers, the majority of airmen who have flown for some months over the lines will ungrudgingly admit that, speaking generally, their opponents have proved themselves worthy foes, not lacking in bravery and "guts." During the last year of the war, their pilots were doubtless inferior to ours in the actual handling of their machines. This was due perhaps to the fact that they were sent to the front less well trained. In shooting we had nothing to learn from them; and our machines were superior in design, whilst week by week we were gaining a superiority in numbers.

In fact, we were becoming more and more "top dog" in the air. No one knew this better than the German airmen, and the knowledge that they were on the losing side cannot but have had a disheartening effect. In the circumstances, they put up a better fight than might have been expected of them.

It has repeatedly been stated that the Hun seldom accepted battle except when numerically superior. After all it is not unnatural that they should attempt to inflict the maximum of loss with the minimum of risk. This trait is by no means peculiar to them. Other arms, on both sides, are averse from searching out their opponent's most formidable positions. If possible, they leave them severely alone, and concentrate on the weak and less adequately protected points.:

In my experience, however, only very rarely have they refused a "scrap" when in numbers approximately equal to our formation. On a few occasions eight to ten scouts have tried conclusions with nine or more of our two-seater fighters. Be it remembered our squadron was one of the most—if not the most—famous on the Western or any front. We had crashed more Hun machines in a month than any other squadron; and when records are published it is at least possible that we may head the list for the period of the war. The Germans, therefore, were under no misapprehension when they engaged us.

Admittedly, it was often glaringly apparent that their pilots lacked confidence in their ability to hold their own with us. They would leisurely come along and mingle with us, displaying a lack of the dash and devil-may-care recklessness so essential in fighting in the air. They often gave me the impression that they were carrying out orders in the ordinary course of duty, which were distasteful to them, and from the performance of which they did not expect to return. Yet they put up a fairly good "show"; and continued to try their strength when, day after day, they had learned from bitter experience that their chances of successfully engaging us were infinitesimal.

There is no doubt that they were keen on shooting down stragglers; but there is, unfortunately, no chivalry of the air which forbids the bagging of a single machine by three or four should the Fortune of War deliver a "lame duck" into their hands. Many of us hope one day to meet some of our late opponents and discuss in a friendly way a thousand and. one things of interest to flying people. It is the opinion of the majority of men who have met them in the air that the German Flying Corps has set an example in "playing the game" to other branches of their army.

Perhaps they also unconsciously tried:—

To set the cause above renown,
To love the game beyond the prize.
To honour, while you strike him down,
The foe that comes with fearless eyes,
To count the Life of Battle good,
And dear the land that gave you birth,
And dearer yet the brotherhood
That binds the brave of all the earth.

As an instance of their occasional audacity in attacking when outnumbered and outclassed I am reminded of how ten of their scouts deliberately sought a fight with twelve of our two-seaters. Their bravery, not to say foolishness, was, needless to say, attended with disastrous results to them.

At about ten o'clock one July morning, after searching in vain for enemy machines from Roulers to Menin, thence to Tourcoing and Roubaix, we had flown over Lille and were following the railway line to the west. The sun was shining brilliantly, and, as is always advisable, I was searching in its rays for the enemy. I saw nothing to arouse my suspicions, and was surprised when a red light was fired from one of the rear machines, the observer of which had spotted a Hun formation in the sun, endeavouring to get close to us without being observed, and had taken immediate steps to inform the rest of us. As a result, we were prepared for the attack.

The Huns dived on us, having a slight advantage in height, but not sufficient to make difficult shooting for our rear guns. They inflicted no material damage on any of our formation, which remained intact—a solid *phalanx* of twenty-four men and guns. It might have been expected that having delivered their attack the Germans would continue their downward course until out of harm's way, lower than we could follow them; this, however, today they did not do, but continued to fight. They were now below the bulk of our formation—ten of them to our twelve. Their outlook was decidedly poor, as we consider ourselves capable of taking on double our number of German scouts; indeed, before the survivors made off, we accounted for no less than five out of the ten. D——— and I had a red-letter day, for we accounted for one each. He, after the preliminary attack, dived on one that made no effort to save itself, but flew calmly on.

After forty to fifty rounds at about 50 yards range she commenced to spin, and was seen by another Pilot to crash on, or near to, the railway line. Shortly afterwards another got under our tail and commenced to shoot at us. I could not at once bring my gun to bear upon her, and had to touch D——— on the right shoulder, whereupon—as per arrangement—he swung the tail over to the right. In the meantime, the Hun had done some fair shooting. There was no time to consider the matter then, but I found afterwards nine bullet holes through the canvas of the cockpit in which I was standing.

How they all missed me is a marvel. Now that I could get my gun upon her, she was a sitting shot, as her speed was much the same as ours. I gave her a magazine of ninety-seven rounds. She waited for no more but rolled over on to her side and ultimately dived vertically to earth.

Shortly after this the scrap was over; and, our time on patrol duty being up, we followed the leader towards home. The fighting had brought us down to a lower altitude than that in which we usually operated. We were at heights varying from 9,000 to 7,000 feet and somewhat spread out. Two machines in fact were about 1,000 yards behind the others when, a couple of miles from the lines, I spotted three biplanes at about 13,000 feet to the rear, and above, our straggling pair. They were larger than scouts and had extensions on the top 'plane, *i.e.,* the latter was longer than the lower plane.

This feature is shared by our machines which spot for the gunners; but whereas they had dihedral—which means that their wings slope downwards towards their junction—the wings of German two-seaters are flat, and parallel with the horizontal. It was evident that they were enemy aircraft—in fact they were Halberstadt two-seaters. They were diving upon our rear machines and I could not be sure that our observers had seen them.

I resolved, therefore, to fire a couple of red lights in order to put them on their guard. There was no time to be wasted; the 3,000 to 6,000 feet between the diving 'planes and ours takes but a short time to reduce to convenient shooting range. I fired one round hastily; loaded again, and pulled the trigger, pointing the pistol to my left front. During the next half minute, I lived many ages, for the burning contents of the cartridge hit the revolving arm of the gun. mounting, and broke into several blazing pieces. The majority went over the side, but a few flew back into my cockpit. These I put out with gauntlets and boots in an incredibly short space of time.

Seldom have I acted more speedily, for the danger was very great that the canvas might light and, fanned by the whirling current of air, cause a fire which could only result in the total destruction of ourselves and the machine. I felt overjoyed when no spark remained, and took a Pyrene Fire Extinguisher from its rack with the object of making doubly certain. Imagine my horror when, some feet down the fuselage, I perceived a large hole in the canvas, around the edges of which flames were slowly eating.

At 8,000 feet with a fire in the fuselage!!! My blood ran cold. I have never been so frightened—so filled with terror. But I must act— and at once. I thanked my lucky stars that I had only the day before recharged the two fire extinguishers which I carried in the cockpit. I had often looked upon them as rather useless *impedimenta*, thinking that they would be no good in case of trouble—that no fire would be sufficiently small for them to cope with—-but they saved the situation, the machine and our lives.

Leaning forward and squeezing my shoulders through the bracing wires, I squirted the chemicals in the direction of the fire. On all sides the liquid was protected from the outer current of air, and so there was no difficulty in bringing it to bear upon the creeping flame. To my relief and joy the fire faded away, and by the time one extinguisher was half exhausted only smouldering canvas and wood remained, and there was no longer any fear of coming down in flames. In the meantime, the German pilots, realising that they had been spotted, had turned their machines towards the east and were rapidly disappearing over Hunland.

CHAPTER 12

Taking the Lead

The squadron had been detailed to provide three offensive patrols. Two formations had already put in their allotted time over the lines, and had been molested by nothing more serious than Archie. Being a bright, sunny day in June, this was distinctly disappointing, for it is on such days that a crack squadron hopes to add materially to its bag of Huns. It was surmised that the latter having been quiescent throughout the morning and afternoon would put up a good "show" in the evening, and that our last patrol might expect a certain amount of "liveliness." his concerned no one more than D—— and myself, owing to the fact that we were to lead the formation.

It was the first time that we had been selected—for this responsible job. We could look back upon the days when, irresponsible and inexperienced, we had criticized—but learned from—veteran leaders. Later, we had been considered capable of taking charge of a group of three, under the supreme direction of a flight commander. By this time, we had realised that fighting the Hun in the air, whilst being vastly entertaining and exciting, is not altogether devoid of risk. It had been impressed upon us that the German Flying Corps is not composed entirely of "dud" pilots, but rather of men capable of putting up a good fight. Last stage of all, we were now to lead a formation of fighting machines.

In passing I may explain that although I have used the term "we" it is the pilot who officially and actually is in charge. As, however, in a two-seater squadron success can only be hoped for where there is a perfect co-operation between pilot and observer, it is natural that the second occupant should wish to be considered not merely ornamental.

The observer in our Air Force—I am speaking of fighting squadrons—must primarily be able to defend the tail, and take advantage of openings his pilot may make for him. He is there to assist the pilot, who must necessarily be in charge and capable of acting on his own initiative at a moment's notice. For him to wait for orders would be fatal. In the German Flying Corps, it is customary for the pilot in a two-seater machine to be a non-commissioned officer—with an officer in the rear cockpit presumably in charge of the machine. Some of their Scout pilots also are non-commissioned officers; who, whatever other qualities they possess, appear to be lacking in that initiative so essential to success in aerial fighting.

Being some years older than D——, who was just nineteen, I felt that I would be able to dissuade him from foolhardy reckless enterprises; and I knew from experience that he was aware that two heads are usually better than one.

The value of a good leader cannot be overestimated. It is not necessary that he has several Huns to his credit; although in practice promotion to flight commander is usually awarded to flying officers who have distinguished themselves in this respect. Sound commonsense and a reputation for "stoutness" is needed rather than fighting brilliancy. There are in all squadrons reckless young daredevils who can be depended upon to account for Huns. In a "scrap" they are magnificent. They need, however, an older, cooler and more calculating head to make opportunities for them.

After taking off we circled round the aerodrome for a time until at 3,500 to 4,000 feet I fired a red light and the formation followed us towards the lines. A succession of green lights informed us that one machine had engine trouble, and had to return, our number being thereby reduced to eleven.

Without further mishap or incident, we approached the war zone and crossed the trenches north of Kemmel Hill, where Archie bade us "welcome." The skies were devoid of hostile aircraft, and we leisurely made for Armentiéres, upon the station of which we had been ordered to drop our bombs. Having disposed of them, we flew towards Lille, keeping directly above the railway line—photographs of which were required, and to procure which my machine had a camera on board.

A large formation of Sopwith Camels had appeared slightly below us when in the vicinity of Armentiéres. They were looking for a "scrap," and made off in another direction and were quickly out of sight. By now I had taken two or three photos of the railway system. This was a very simple matter; flying as we were at 15,000 feet it was only necessary to go through a couple of mechanical movements every seventy-five seconds. At the same time, it had been assiduously searching the skies for enemy machines. A surprise attack was the last thing I desired on this—our first leading "show."

But the Fates decreed otherwise. In the early mornings the Hun, flying from his aerodromes with the sun behind him, persistently tried to hide in its rays until within shooting range of our patrols. In the evenings, on the other hand, it is we who have the sun behind us. But, on this occasion, a wily leader had manoeuvred round until his convoy was not only in the sun, but between us and our own lines— rather unusual presumption on the enemy's part.

My first intimation that we were being attacked was the sudden appearance of circular, revolving wisps of tracer smoke. A moment later five Fokker Biplanes were clearly defined as leaving their haven of concealment, they were outlined against the limpid blue of the evening sky. One and all of our formation had been surprised—a fact which furnishes ample proof of the value of the sun in aerial warfare.

There was no need to inform the others that a state of "liveliness" existed. The rear machines had been attacked from their right flank. The remainder wheeled about and raced independently to take part in the "scrap." This, unfortunately, was of short duration. Three of our machines were shot about—one somewhat badly, and had to be nursed home. Of the attackers one was shot down by an observer. The surviving four being hopelessly outnumbered, and having lost the initial advantage of height and invisibility, dived away towards Hunland.

We pursued them for a while, but as they displayed an exceptional turn of speed had, perforce, to give up the chase. Besides, as we were already a considerable distance over the lines, to have been lured still further afield held out possibilities of disaster in the face of vastly superior numbers, or of being forced to make an ignominious landing owing to our supply of petrol becoming exhausted. We had to remember that a breeze of from 30 to 40 miles per hour was accelerating our progress towards the east.

I fired a number of red lights with the object of collecting the formation, and D—— turned towards the lines, making a detour of Armentiéres so as to evade the majority of Archie batteries in and about the town. In this we were far from successful. We had underestimated the range of the latest enemy anti-aircraft guns.

We were flying very slowly, so as to give our followers time to sort themselves out and take up their original positions. As a result, we offered a more than usually easy target for the discriminating Bosche gunners. Their marksmanship was distinctly good. The *"wouff, wouff"* of shells at a convenient distance was quickly followed by the ominous *"krunch, krunch"* of those unpleasantly near. There was no alternative to "sticking it." The urgent necessity for collecting the formation prevented us from taking the usual steps to shake off the menace.

A variation to Archie's discordant music was suddenly provided by the *hiss-s-s-s* of flying fragments, followed by a deep-throated cough from immediately below. The machine shivered and for a moment appeared undecided as to the course she intended to pursue. Ultimately righting herself she continued serenely on. I was at that time standing up so as to be in a position to see all that was transpiring. My right hand was—as always when over Hunland—grasping the spade grip of my Lewis gun.

Glancing down I saw that both gun and gloved hand were covered with ice. As I looked round D—— switched off the engine and told me that a chunk of Archie had gone through the water jacket. He pointed at the same time to the remnants of the glass vane in front of him. It had been shattered by a piece of metal. On further investigation several punctures were discernible in the wings, whilst two large holes had been made in the fuselage two or three feet in front of me.

There was no doubt as to our immediate course of action. Without any delay we must make for our side of the lines, and try to reach an aerodrome before the engine "seized up" and made a forced landing necessary. The formation was straggling somewhat a few hundred yards to our rear. I fired some green lights to inform the second leader that we had to return home, and that he must take charge of the patrol. The temporary indecision of our machine had been noticed by him, and for a moment the backward rush of icy water had given him the impression that we were likely to go down in flames. He decided to escort us to within a reasonable distance of the lines. This secured us immunity from roving Huns and from undivided attention by Archie.

Our engine—a Rolls-Royce—in which we had implicit faith, did not "let us down," and a quarter of an hour later we had landed on an aerodrome. In response to a 'phone message to our squadron, skilled mechanics arrived with commendable promptitude; and in a few hours we had once again a thoroughly serviceable machine.

Two days later we again led a formation of twelve machines. This expedition, unlike the last, was, somewhat to our relief, productive of no thrilling, exciting incidents. Nothing out of the ordinary occurred. We patrolled well over the German side of the lines for the allotted period of 1½ hours, but without sighting a hostile machine. The reason for this was that the ground being obscured by clouds, the British Air Force had a "walk-over"; as on such occasions the German airmen sit at home and—as is the wont of flying men—pray that "dud" days may be plentiful.

Perhaps their high command console themselves for the inactivity of their juniors by the knowledge that with no visibility we are unable to obtain that for which we exist—namely, information. This theory is doubtless in the main correct, although there have been times when unexpected and temporary breaks in the clouds have revealed matters of more than passing interest.

Inability to see the objective did not interfere with the daily delivery of bombs. As on fine days, every machine on an Offensive Patrol carried one or more. Two-seaters were laden with an "egg" weighing 112 lb., and scouts with two or more 20-pounders. Our objective today was Estaires. As no "hot air" patches favoured us; we had to steer by compass, whilst at the same time remembering the mileage to be covered and the effect of wind on our progress. It is highly improbable that Estaires received material damage: but the moral effect of bombs arriving at all hours, apparently from dense clouds, must on such days have been prodigious, and not without its influence on the troops scattered throughout the back of the German front.

Before proceeding further, I would warn readers that if they wish to read of war, they should skip the remainder of this chapter. For a while the battlefield is obscured, both literally and metaphorically, by a flawless covering of clouds. At one time, indeed, two layers—possessing the most divergent attributes—separated us from Mother Earth.

It happened in this way. On setting off, shortly after lunch, to patrol the lines, it was noticed that clouds were massing over Hunland—some 20 miles away. Momentarily reinforcements were arriving from the west, and it was conjectured that by the time we arrived over the battle zone observation would be impossible.

By the time we had climbed to 5,000 feet, small white clouds were, it seemed, sorting themselves out, getting into position, and generally making themselves ready to proceed eastwards in support of those already in action.

Within our immediate range little fleecy cloud creations were bestirring themselves, and joining issue with the main body in process of formation over Hunland. This type of cloud-form was, at the time, new, to me. Nor have I since seen anything of the same nature at such a low altitude. They were exceedingly tiny, if such a term may be applied to clouds, and gave one the impression of being very delicate and of gossamer-like texture. My thoughts were, involuntarily, carried back to a New Zealand sheep station, where I had seen fleeces of the finest Merino wool spread out after washing on the grass to dry.

I saw, too, in imagination once more, raw cotton in a Calcutta mill—but here the material was less white, and of a coarser texture. By the time we had reached the trenches neither they nor the devastated area could be seen. The cloud forms, some larger than others, but all absurdly small, had fraternised and formed a solid barrier.

The scene by now was a magnificent one. The sun far above gave to the whole surface a radiant, golden, shimmering appearance. It was as if the most flawless fleeces of the world's flocks had been marshalled for inspection by their Lord the Sun, who, well pleased, was bestowing -upon them his benediction. We were not permitted to look upon this scene of beauty for long. Another and equally impressive tableau was in process of formation. The fleecy cloud layer was moving slowly towards the east at 3,000 feet above the earth. We were at 12,000 feet, and between us and them massive forms of purest white were being ushered by the wind's behests to their predestined place in the day's scheme of things.

Presently the lower layer was completely hidden from view and we were at liberty to drink in every detail of the newly arrived cloud country. But it is, unfortunately, far beyond me to provide words by which the glories displayed may be described.

I hope one day to see the Rocky Mountains, and a trip to Switzerland is a pleasure reserved for the first year of Peace. In my wanderings, however, I have many times seen the Himalayan dawn from Darjeeling; and on one occasion have witnessed from Tiger Hill the supreme scene when the sun, rising in majesty, lifts up and disperses from the valleys encircling Mount Everest the mists which have lain dormant throughout the dark hours.

For a few moments before their orderly departure, they are suffused with a radiance of many and varied tints, of which glistening gold prevails on the topmost forms whilst a film of pink partially obscures those lying at a lower level. To such a scene may be compared with advantage that which I am trying to describe. But whereas these Eastern mists are part only of a radiant spectacle, this fills the whole scene, and stretches as far as the eye can reach—to all semblance to the utmost ends of the earth.

It occurred to me that could the wild, rugged, mountainous tracts of Zululand be clothed in cloud-forms, the transformation would closely resemble this glorious expanse where *kopjes*, mountains and valleys were thrown together in riotous, reckless, yet natural profusion. It was easy to picture in imagination native *kraals* on the hill tops, roads circling round the mountains, and water courses winding through the valleys.

Over this land of wonder and mystery we flew, viewing country fated to exist but for a short time. Yet to those who love the wild places of Earth, it is consolatory to realise that ever new and wonderful creations of unsurpassable beauty succeed one another in the Realms of the Air.

CHAPTER 13

Lessons Learned

The preceding chapters were written some months ago—before and after the Armistice.

Now that they are about to be published a few friends have asked me to write a short *précis* giving the lessons I have learned and the conclusions I have arrived at as a result of my experiences in aerial warfare. They have pointed out that in spite of the publication of many flying books, the war has produced little or nothing to which the next generation of youthful aviators can refer for some slight guidance in their study of war flying. Very unwillingly I have consented, being fully aware that the subject is one to which no single flying officer can hope to do justice. Also being an observer, I must treat it only from the point of view of that fraternity, whose problems and difficulties I will endeavour to describe.

Offensive patrols usually comprised from six to twelve machines. It will perhaps be as well, therefore; before proceeding further to narrate the events which led to the adoption and the development of formation flying. To do so will be to give a brief history of the R.F.C. and R.A.F. during the war.

In the first place it is of more than passing interest to note that—contrary to the general belief—fighting in the air was looked upon previous to August, 1914, as a contingency to be reckoned with in the next campaign.

The following is an extract from the *Manual* of the R.F.C., which was published early in 1914:—

It is probable that one phase of the struggle for the command of the air will resolve itself into a series of combats between individual aeroplanes or pairs of aeroplanes. If the pilots of one side can succeed in obtaining victory in a succession of such combats, they will establish a moral ascendancy over the surviving pilots of the enemy and be left free to carry out their duties of reconnaissance. The actual tactics adopted must depend on the types of the aeroplanes engaged, the object of the pilot being to obtain for his passenger the free use of his own weapon, while denying to the enemy the use of his. To disable the pilot of the opposing aeroplane will be the first object. In the case of fast reconnaissance aeroplanes, it will often be advisable to avoid fighting, in order to carry out a mission or to deliver information, but it must be borne in mind that this will sometimes be impossible, and that, as in every other class of fighting, a fixed determination to attack and win will be the surest road to victory.

Had the war been over at the end of 1915 the above would have been an excellent prophecy of the conditions that would then obtain—namely, combats between single aeroplanes or pairs of aeroplanes manned by the pilot flying the machine with an armed observer as passenger.

In August, 1914, we possessed no machines with fighting capacity. With the exception of a few single-seater scouts the majority were two-seater B.E.'s (British Experimental) capable of doing 65 miles per hour. Until the advent of trench warfare practically the sole duty of the R.F.C. was reconnaissance. It was a scout that brought back the information that General—Smith-Dorrien was faced by three army corps and not by three divisions as had been thought. Had this knowledge not been obtained French's "contemptible little army" would very possibly have been completely annihilated. This incident tends to show how different a role, aeroplanes might have played had the war remained one of movement.

On settling down to trench warfare the Germans at once commenced spotting for their artillery. They had more machines, better engines and a more highly trained personnel than did their opponents. We followed their example, the lack of a sufficient number of serviceable aeroplanes being less felt than if we had possessed a larger supply of ammunition.

Archie being almost unknown in those days, machines were perfectly safe when out of range of rifle and machine-gun fire from the ground. Both sides carried on with their work unmolested. There was nothing to prevent our pilots and observers from doing reconnaissances and spotting for the guns and *vice versa*.

Naturally this state of affairs could not continue, since if two armies are equally well supplied with information the one of the other, the nett result is nil; while the main role of the flying arm is to act as "the eyes of the army" *whilst denying to the enemy the use of his*. Enterprising pilots and observers therefore commenced to experiment with grenades and bombs. Others took up rifles or revolvers and by a combination of luck and judgment a few machines were brought down. This was the birth of fighting in the air.

It is interesting to note that in the early days German machines were, on more than one occasion, driven down by mere moral superiority; in other words, they were forced to land without a shot being fired, apparently mesmerised by the terrifying stunts of our pilots.

After we had armed, our "gun buses," *i.e.*, Vickers "Pushers," Henry and Morris Farmans, with machine-guns, the Germans were the first to instal them on "tractors." One of our machines drove down one of the latter so armed, although our pilot had nothing more than a revolver. Our machine was badly shot about, but the pilot dived so closely on the tail of the Hun that the latter was forced to break off the combat.

From March, 1915, machine-guns were installed in all machines. The B.E. was, however, not well suited for this work, as the observer was situated in a small cockpit with the planes above and below him, the propeller in front and the pilot behind—a position which, though suitable for observation of the ground, was quite unsuitable either for seeing other aeroplanes in the air or for the effective use of machine guns.

Aeroplanes of the "Pusher" type were therefore produced, in which both the pilot and observer had an excellent field of view and of fire to the front, while the observer, by standing up and facing towards the tail, could bring his gun to bear on an enemy in rear. The best known of this type was the F.E. (Fighting Experimental), of which both two-seaters and scouts were sent to the front.

At about this period—the concluding months of 1915—the Germans brought out the famous Fokker Monoplane Scout. This was the first type of machine—enemy or Allied—in which the problem of shooting through the propeller was satisfactorily solved. This gave the enemy an enormous advantage. With its aid he made a bold bid to gain a definite supremacy in the air and with a considerable measure of success. Such havoc was wrought amongst the B.E.'s that they became known as "Fokker-fodder." The Fokker pilots' plan was to make one dive on an artillery machine, pour a stream of lead into her and, whether successful or not, make his way back over Hunland.

Not being by any means a handy machine, however, our pilots found that by turning at the critical moment they could avoid his fire whilst giving their observer a chance of retaliation. Yet, it must be admitted they were a decided nuisance. To combat them we were compelled to adopt the plan of sending out machines in pairs—one to do the work whilst the other watched the skies for a surprise attack. The Germans replied to this by sending out two or more attackers. Thus, the Fokker was directly responsible for the initial stage of formation flying.

In the meantime, our designers had not been idle. Early in 1916 the R.F.C. in the field was vastly strengthened by the arrival of several Squadrons of machines built solely for fighting. The D.H.2 Scout (a De Havilland production) turned out to be more than a match for the Fokker, whilst an improved type of F.E. Pusher two-seater did splendid work. No praise is too high for the personnel manning the latter. Being handicapped by being unable to defend the tail of their machine, they adopted the plan when attacked of flying round and round in circles.

Thus, each observer defended the tail of the machine immediately in front of him. With the advent of these squadrons, we more than held our own in the air, which we continued to do throughout the war, until at the cessation of hostilities the Royal Air Force had a very distinct ascendancy over the aerial forces of the enemy.

As the R.F.C. was numerically in a strong the escort system and to substitute that of patrols. Each squadron was allotted certain periods of the day in which it was its duty to protect our artillery machines and prevent those of the enemy from doing their allotted jobs.

This system continued uninterruptedly throughout the war. The Germans adopted the same plan, and aerial combats in which a dozen or more machines were engaged became a common occurrence. As more machines were sent out any hour of the day found more and still more fighting 'planes in the air until aerial fighting, which had commenced with individual duels, developed into battles in which 100 or more machines were engaged.

Doubtless, our flying men got the better of the enemy in the great majority of these encounters. It must not be forgotten, however, that the success of fighting squadrons was measured by an army commander more by the good work which our artillery was enabled to do, and the inaccuracy of the enemy's gunners, than by the number of Huns crashed in aerial combat.

It is not my intention to follow the development of the various types of scouts, but rather to pass on to the arrival of that unmatched fighting machine—the Bristol Fighter. The two-seater F.E.'s had done exceptionally good work. As I have before remarked, however, they were handicapped by the observer's field of fire to the rear being cut off by the planes and propeller.

In addition, it was a comparatively simple matter for a skilled enemy pilot to approach unseen. Now that shooting through the propeller was a *fait accompli* it is only natural that designers concentrated on a fighting tractor machine in which the pilot sat in front and the observer was placed behind to defend the tail.

Squadrons equipped with Bristol Fighters commenced to arrive in France early in 1917, from which time until the conclusion of the campaign they were recognised as second to none in maintaining our ascendancy in the air.

It may be of interest here to give a few examples of types of formation that have been tried at various stages of the war and under varying conditions.

No. 1.   The Three-pair Type.
This was simply an extension of the " escort "
system.

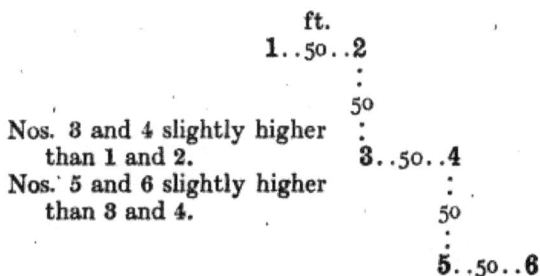

ft.
1..50..2
:
50
:
Nos. 3 and 4 slightly higher :
than 1 and 2.   3..50..4
Nos. 5 and 6 slightly higher   :
than 3 and 4.   50
:
5..50..6

If one of a pair was damaged or for any reason had to retire from the Patrol the other accompanied her. This type did not long survive.

No. 2. The Diamond Type.

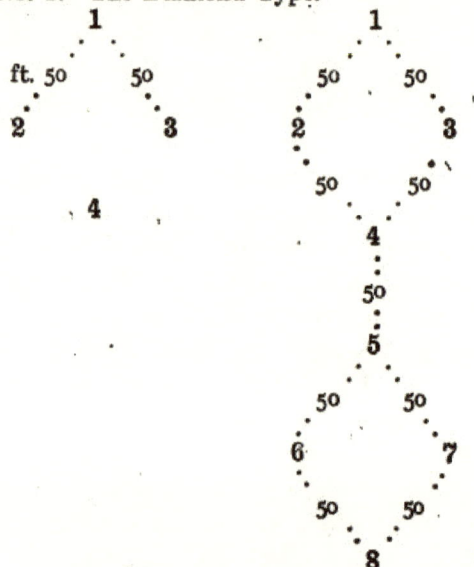

```
        1                           1
   ·  ·  ·                      ·  ·  ·
ft. 50      50              50      50
  ·            ·          ·            ·
  2            3          2            3
                            ·        · \
                            50      50
                              ·    ·
                                4
                                ·
                                ·
                               50
                                ·
                                5
                                ·
                            50      50
                          ·            ·
                          6            7
                            ·        ·
                            50      50
                              ·    ·
                                8
```

As in the three-pair system all machines flew at
a greater elevation than those immediately in
front of them.

No. 3. 2nd Brigade Type.

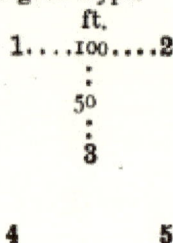

```
              ft.
        1....100....2
              :
             50
              :
              3


        4           5
              ·
```

This was found to be very useful when taking
photographs in the face of opposition. No. 3
had the camera and flew somewhat lower than
his escort.

No. 4. The V Type.
This is the formation that was most generally used. It was always employed by our Squadron in 1917 and 1918.

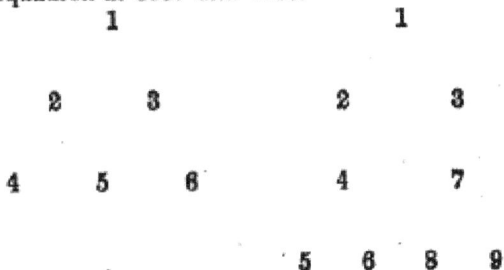

```
        1                           1

   2         3               2           3

 4      5       6          4         7

                        5    6    8    9
```

This formation has been described in Chapter 1. With twelve machines the remaining three "sat" up above slightly to the rear to guard against attack from the skies.

In formation flying the responsibility of the leader is immense. No rash daredevil is suitable for this, the most important job in aerial warfare. What is needed is a cool, calm, unexcitable man who, whilst missing no favourable opportunities, will not endanger the existence of his followers by taking unduly grave risks. I remember one day on returning from a patrol listening to the laments of a hot-headed youngster who could not understand why the leader had not led us to attack a patrol of Fokker Biplanes over Lille. He had seen them and was sure they were enemy scouts. Needless to say, the leader had also spotted them, but he was much too wily to be drawn so far from home. Had he done so the wind, which usually favoured the Germans, would have necessitated the ignominious landing of twelve machines on the wrong side of the line.

A leader must realise that the time must be taken from the slowest machine just as in the infantry or cavalry by the least speedy man or horse. In every formation there must necessarily be pilots with comparatively little experience of flying, and still less of fighting, and to outpace them is to play into the hands of any "jackals" that may be hovering in the skies.

It is his business to keep the formation compact and therefore in a position to make the most of any opportunities that may arise for offensive action. At the same time, he must so manoeuvre when attacked in overwhelming numbers that the attackers receive the benefit of the full broadside from all units of the formation. He may rest assured that if his followers have faith in him, they will follow him to hell if need be. On the other hand, if he is a man of weak character, vacillating and undecided, the morale of the patrol will be visibly affected and disaster is likely to. follow. Be it remembered that in spite of our undoubted ascendancy in the air offensive patrols were not picnics, nor did the German Flying Corps Staff approve of pleasure cruises over their domains.

An example of the inevitable result of losing formation is given in the third chapter. The sky might be clear of Huns, but if a single machine got isolated, they would appear apparently from nowhere. There were times innumerable when, owing to engine trouble or some other cause, one of the patrol had to leave the formation and make for the lines. The majority reached an aerodrome safely; but there were others who did not. There was in most squadrons no arrangement made for the escorting of a "lame duck" out of the danger zone. To make matters worse, it was usual to fire a green light to inform the leader of one's departure.

Of course, the enemy knew the meaning of that light and acted accordingly. It was better to creep away without giving any intimation to the flight commander. His observer should be able to keep him informed of the movements of his patrol without extraneous aid. It would perhaps have been-more satisfactory if it had been an understood thing that on a green light being fired, the whole patrol should escort the "lame duck" to within a reasonable distance of the trenches. There were times when this could not be done, as, for instance, when the leader had his eye on a patrol of Huns. In the majority of cases, however, it could have been without impairing in any way the efficient performance of the duties of the formation.

It has been suggested that a single machine should have acted as escort to one falling out, but this meant a weakening of the patrol without improving matters materially for the "lame duck," as the "jackals" usually operated in fives or sixes.

In Chapter 7 it may be remembered my pilot and I left a "scrap" because we had not a single available gun. As a result, we nearly "bought it," both from Archie and from Pfalz Scouts. Were I ever again in the same predicament my counsel would be to climb above the formation. There we could "sit" until the Huns were defeated.

Given a good leader and a compact formation an observer was left free to concentrate all his attention on Huns in the air. To be of real assistance to his pilot he had firstly to be able to distinguish foes from friends, and secondly to be able to shoot straight when the former arrived within range.

As to the first of these requirements most beginners found it extremely difficult to distinguish one type from another. I am referring now more particularly to 1917. In 1918 when Pfalz Scouts and Fokker Biplanes, with extensions on their top wings, largely superseded our old friends the Albatrii matters were vastly simplified. After some experience one got to know enemy machines and to sense their presence almost instinctively. It was quite a common occurrence for our own or allied machines to be fired upon by the inexperienced. Several instances of such mistaken identity occur to me. On my second offensive patrol two scouts sat on my tail, creeping nearer every moment. An expert would have known them at once as Belgian Nieuports. I didn't, and becoming suspicious decided to take no risks and fired a burst between them. One of them immediately lifted a wing and showed her markings.

On another occasion a formation of French *Breguets* passed at right angles to us—1,000 yards or more to the rear of our formation. A new observer in the machine on my right merrily rattled through a magazine in spite of my frantic signals backed up by a white Very light fired in his direction.

Once again one day when my pilot was leading the formation, we sighted a patrol of scouts going eastward from the direction of Merville. We inclined towards them to see what British Squadron it was. They had bright red tails and looked in the distance somewhat Hunnish. On closer inspection they turned out to be Dolphins—a type which had recently come to that sector of the line. No less than three observers fired at them—luckily at a quite impossible range. Nor could they be afterwards persuaded that they were British machines, and think to this day that we missed the chance of our lives in not diving on them and shooting them down.

Squadron Offices in France used to contain innumerable silhouettes of enemy machines by the study of which a beginner could supplement his practical work in the air. Now that there is time to train flying officers very thoroughly for the next war, doubtless more attention will be given to this important point. No pilot or observer should consider himself fit for war service until he can tell at a glance—at ever increasing distances, the type of an approaching machine. Training centres will presumably possess aeroplanes of all nationalities, and

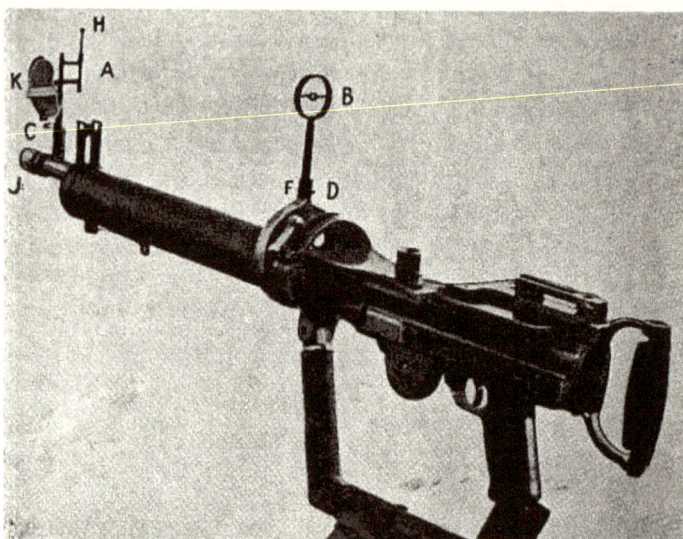

SHOWING RING BACK-SIGHT AND WIND-PANEL FORE-SIGHT
(NORMAN PATTERN).

classes for instruction in identification of types will perhaps be a feature of the new training curriculum.

Now we come to the second requirement, namely, good shooting, in which must be included the care of the machine-gun. "*A good workman always takes care of his tools*"—which applied to aerial fighting means that neglect to look after one's gun results in a jamb at a critical moment with its attendant possibilities.

In my squadron there appeared one day a somewhat elderly man. He did not consider himself old, but he was only a few months junior to the C.O. who was thirty-two—and so much older than the "children" under his command. This old man suddenly found himself famous. Visitors from other squadrons were anxious to meet the enthusiast who, it was said, turned out before dawn, religiously took his Lewis gun to pieces and put it together again, inserting always new spare parts. It was reported that the early morning "show" used to be awakened by him testing his gun outside the huts.

I am afraid the story was somewhat exaggerated. The subject of it is, however, alive to tell the tale, and so does not regret having supplied entertainment to the finest might of the best squadron of the war.

The moral is obvious. It is quite impossible for an observer (or a pilot) to take too much care of his gun.

If you contemplate fighting a duel, it is as well to make sure that your pistol is capable of backing you up. So, in the air against the Hun. No praise can be too high for the armourers who looked after our weapons. But it was our lives—not theirs—that were at stake. Neglect to change at very frequent intervals extractors and cartridge guide springs has very possibly been the cause of a number of names appearing in the list of "missing."

As regards actual shooting—the *sine qua non* of a fighting aviator—there is no need to drive home the point that it is impossible to have too much practice. An observer must be able to do everything connected with his gun without conscious thought, so that all his mental energies may be concentrated on the Hun or Huns. Changing parts and making minor repairs in the air have to be done practically instinctively, undisturbed by the formidable distractions of machine-gun fire from close quarters. He must be able to place the enemy machine in the correct position in the ring (B) (Photograph illustrating Lewis Gun and Sights, *vide* opposite page).

With the theory of the ring-sight I have no intention of afflicting the reader. From the practical point of view, however, it must be pointed out that to hit a machine in the air it is necessary to aim in front just as in partridge or pheasant shooting. But as it is impossible to estimate correctly and quickly in dozens of feet this sight was introduced. It is designed for a speed of 100 miles per hour and at 200 yards allows for 362 feet for a machine flying at right angles to the line of fire, when the outer edge of the ring should cut the pilot's seat. A machine approaching must be placed inside the ring, and the smaller the angle of approach the nearer the centre must it be placed until in the case of a Hun directly on one's tail the centre of the ring and the bead (H) are in line with the nose of the Bosche machine.

The observer's task has been vastly simplified since the commencement of aerial fighting when nothing but the ordinary **V** sight was available. Now, in addition to the ring-sight there is a compensating foresight (K), which compensates for the speed of one's own machine; also, a proportion of the bullets used are tracers which give an approximate idea of the course they are taking.

Still another valuable aid lies in the use of the ring-sight as a distance judger. Roughly speaking, a German scout at 400 yards overlapped the bead and at 300 yards the inner ring, whilst at 200 yards it half-filled and at 100 yards completely filled the outer ring.

Much ammunition was wasted during the war by observers firing at impossible ranges. When it is-remembered that at 250 yards an average gunner will in the air spread his shots over a circle of about 30 feet diameter or 15 feet radius round the pilot, one realises the absurdity of firing, as was often done, at 1,000 yards or more. When acting strictly on the defensive it may be permissible, as your opponents are informed that you are on the alert. When on the offensive it simply means using up rounds that may be sorely needed later, besides taking the chance of getting a jam and so being out of action when the Hun gets to close quarters.

Unless the enemy is making good shooting on your machine it appears best to reserve your fire until he comes within 200 yards; above all it is useless depending on "tracers" at ranges over 100 yards. At under that range it is quite another matter, and instead of bursts of ten or more rounds, one may now turn the gun on as if it were a garden hose.

If an observer of a fighting machine can distinguish types of machines and get in good shooting, he has mastered the elementary but necessary matters that go towards success in aerial fighting.

There is another important point that must not be overlooked. He must possess an eye for country. This is inborn in some who, like carrier pigeons, invariably find their way home. Men from the dominions seldom lost themselves. They had been used to wide, open spaces. Others from large cities found it more difficult rapidly to acquire a knowledge of the country over which they flew. It should be a point of honour never to get lost.

There were innumerable cases of machines landing scores of miles from their aerodrome even on a perfectly clear day. In dull, cloudy weather there was some excuse for this, but after a while one should be able to pick up one's whereabouts through a momentary break in the clouds. An excellent reason for taking pains to learn the geography of the country lay in the fact that without such knowledge one was in a quandary when claiming a Hun as having crashed; of this proof was required, and to endeavour to obtain confirmation of a machine believed to have crashed near Staden was perfectly futile if the crash actually occurred in Ledeghem, some miles away.

Last of all we come to that all-important factor—co-operation between pilot and observer. It was no easy matter during the war for a squadron commander to decide with whom a new observer should fly, and *vice versa*. An experienced pilot with a new and perhaps somewhat "dud" observer would always, if the worst came to the worst, ignore his passenger and temporarily imagine himself to be flying a single seater. On the other hand, an old observer was by no means keen on flying with an unknown quantity. The only alternative was to send two new men up together and hope for the best.

Eventually every useful observer paired off with a pilot with whom he would invariably fly. Not only that, but in many cases, they would become, like David and Jonathan, inseparable during the intervals of flying. Thus, they got to know one another intimately, and as a result became very dependable and useful.

Now that all R.A.F. officers are to learn to fly, a two-seater will presumably be manned by two pilots who will be equally at home in the front or the back seat. This opens out great possibilities for school friends who, if allowed to train as cadets together and fly in company permanently, should form an irresistible combination. There is another form of co-operation which must be mentioned, namely that between flying officers and the men who look after their machines and guns. The pride that mechanics took in their charges was, during the war, immense. They were proud of the reputation of their squadrons, flights and individual machines.

Visitors would be shown planes which had accounted for Huns, and long and earnest were the discussions in messes as to the relative merits of the various squadrons and their personnel. At busy times whilst flyers were having well-earned rest mechanics would be up night after night, denying themselves sleep, in order that machines might be in perfect condition for operations. No praise can be too high for the work done by N.C.O.'s and men on active service. They brought an expert knowledge combined with a zeal and enthusiasm which went far towards the success of the Air Services in the Great War.

Aeroplane Design

Frank Barnwell in the cockpit

Contents

A Foreword

By C. G. Grey, editor of "The Aeroplane"

So many new firms are now entering the Aeroplane Industry, and in consequence so many trained engineers are for the first time taking a serious interest in aeronautical engineering that the time seems opportune to publish a general review of the general principles of aeroplane design.

The disquisition on the subject, which follows this preface, was originally written by Mr. F. S. Barnwell to be read as a paper before the Engineering Society of Glasgow University. It was subsequently published in serial form in *The Aeroplane* early in 1915, and so great and so constant was the demand for the numbers containing the treatise that it has seemed worthwhile to republish the whole in the form of a small book. Mr. Barnwell's remarks on design as such will be easily understood by any constructional engineer, and his references to questions of stability will doubtless be made more understandable to those engineers who have not hitherto studied aerodynamics by Mr. Sayers' simple explanation of the why, wherefore, and how of stable aeroplanes.

It seems well to make clear why this writer should be taken seriously by trained and experienced engineers, especially in these days when aeronautical science is in its infancy, and when much harm has been done both to the development of aeroplanes and to the good repute of genuine aeroplane designers by people who pose as " aeronautical experts " on the strength of being able to turn out strings of incomprehensible calculations resulting from empirical formulae based on debatable figures acquired from inconclusive experiments carried out by persons of doubtful reliability on instruments of problematic accuracy.

Certain British manufacturers of sufficient independence of character have proceeded along their own lines and have produced aeroplanes which remain unbeaten, power for power, by any in the world on the score of sheer efficiency. These machines—notably Avro two-seater "tractor" biplanes, Bristol single seater biplane Scouts, Martinsyde Scouts, and Vicker's "pusher" gun-carrier biplanes—have done more than anything else to assure to the Royal Flying Corps during 1915 that ascendancy in the air over German aircraft which has been such a notable feature of the war.

Among these machines the speediest of all up to the end of 1915 was the Bristol Scout, a tiny tractor biplane designed in 1914 by Mr. F. S. Barnwell (now a Captain, R.F.C.), with the practical help of Mr. Harry Busteed, an Australian aviator, now an officer of the Royal Naval Air Service, and at that time in the employ of the Bristol Co.

The fact that the writing was done before the war acquits Mr. Barnwell of any charge of dabbling with the pen contrary to military custom, and his consent to read the proofs of this reprint was only prompted by the instinct of self-defence.

It is to be noted that his general method of design is approved by other aeroplane designers who have been successful in producing efficient and effective aeroplanes. Consequently, the new arrival in the aircraft industry may take it that he is fairly safe in following that method.

C. G. G.

Preface

Written November, 1915.

The contents of this small book originated as a paper which was read to the Glasgow University Engineering Society in the winter of 1914.

They were published during January and February by my friend, Mr. C. G. Grey, in his paper *The Aeroplane*, without any alterations or amendments.

Since Mr. Grey has considered it worth republishing in book form, I have, at his request, gone over the proofs and made sundry alterations and deletions, most of small moment.

The reader must bear in mind, therefore, that the figures and constants quoted remain those which seemed reasonable at the time of first writing the Paper.

One or two clerical errors have been corrected, a fair amount of unnecessary verbiage cut out, the empirical formula for Rudder Area (see Directional Stability) altered, and the figures for Dihedral angle (see Lateral Stability) slightly amplified.

I regret that it has not been possible for me to re-write entirely the sections on Lateral and Directional Stability, for these are treated all too scantily and inaccurately even in comparison with the rest of work.

The original "Preliminary Remarks" and "Conclusion" are left in, practically unaltered, for the excuses and apologies contained therein are still more necessary now than when the Paper was first written.

F. S. Barnwell.

Bristol, 9 Nov., 1915.

Error.—In Fig. 12, (see Longitudinal Stability), the Reaction on the Tail is shown as a downward force; this is, of course, a mistake, as it would be an upward one for the flight path shown. It has not been altered as this would incur making a new block, and it does not affect the explanation of the method.

Part 1: Preliminary Remarks

Before starting on my subject matter, I wish to make some excuses and apologies which I trust the reader will accept. Aeroplane engineering is a young science about which most people know very little; whilst those of us who do think we know something about it do not know nearly as much as we should like to. So, to take a small sub-division of aeroplane design and attempt to deal with it accurately and fully would probably be of less interest to the majority than to attempt a sort of precis of the whole subject.

Hence in this brief work I try to deal with a very large subject in a manner necessarily distinctly sketchy. Now it is hard, when one must be brief, to touch on all essential points, to be lucid and to be academically accurate. It takes as much time trying to work out how to express oneself sufficiently fully, accurately, and yet briefly as to plod straight on saying everything one knows, or thinks one knows, about a subject, and, unfortunately, I have not been able to give nearly as much time as I should have liked to the working out, altering and correcting of this paper. Asking your indulgence therefore for what may be obscure, for what may be incorrect, and for what may be tedious, I shall commence on my subject.

I shall start by briefly describing of what we shall consider an aeroplane to consist, limiting my description to 3 types (see Figs, (1a), (2a), and (3a)).

An aeroplane we shall consider therefore as a machine consisting of a closed-in body in which is a seat for the pilot and (in machines other than single-seaters) a seat or seats for a passenger or passengers. In this body are also the control mechanisms for the motor and for the movable surfaces of the machine. Mounted in or on this body are the tanks for fuel and lubricant. Mounted on either the fore or aft end of this body is the motor, the only type presently worth considering being the petrol internal combustion. Directly coupled to the motor is an air propeller. Attached to the body are the main lifting surfaces, or, as I shall henceforth call them, "Aerofoils." Attached to the underside of the body is the landing gear. Attached to the rear end of the body is the tail, consisting of a fixed part called the tail plane, and a movable portion (or portions) called the elevator (or elevators); also attached to the rear end of the body are the movable vertical rudder and (if any) a fixed vertical surface or rear fin.

This applies, of course, to the case in which the engine and propeller are fixed to the fore end of the fuselage (as in Figs. *1a* and *2a*). If (as in Fig. *3a*) the engine and propeller are at the rear end of the fuselage, then the tail rudder and fin must be attached to suitable outriggers, which are clear of the propeller disc.

You will note that I have described only the direct-driven "tractor" monoplane and biplane, and the direct-driven "pusher" biplane. I think that at present these three types contain the greatest number of desirable features, and it is not advisable in the scope of this paper to discuss further types, however tempting their points for future development may appear.

It is necessary to consider now the functioning of an aeroplane in the simplest conditions and to arrive at the primary necessities for the machine's fulfilling these conditions. Let us consider an aeroplane of total weight, WT, travelling at some uniform velocity VI, in a straight line and horizontally (Fig. 1).

The forces acting on this machine are (1) its weight vertically downwards, (2) total "lift" of whole machine vertically upwards (note here that I say advisedly of "whole" machine), (3) thrust of air propeller in and along direction of flight, (4) total head-resistance of whole machine in and opposite to direction of flight.

For the maintenance of this condition of straight horizontal flight it is obvious that at this speed VI, total "lift" of machine must be equal to total weight, and propeller thrust must be equal to total head resistance. Further, if, as is most probable, the line of action of total head resistance does not coincide with that of thrust, then the C.G. (centre of gravity) of the whole machine must be such a distance in front of the line of action of total lift if thrust be below head resistance, or behind if thrust be above head resistance, that the weight-lift couple is equal to, and of opposite sign to, the thrust-head-resistance couple. In an ideal design, thrust, head-resistance, and lift should all pass through the C.G. and they generally do so approximately. But if it be impossible to attain this, it is preferable that thrust should be kept as nearly

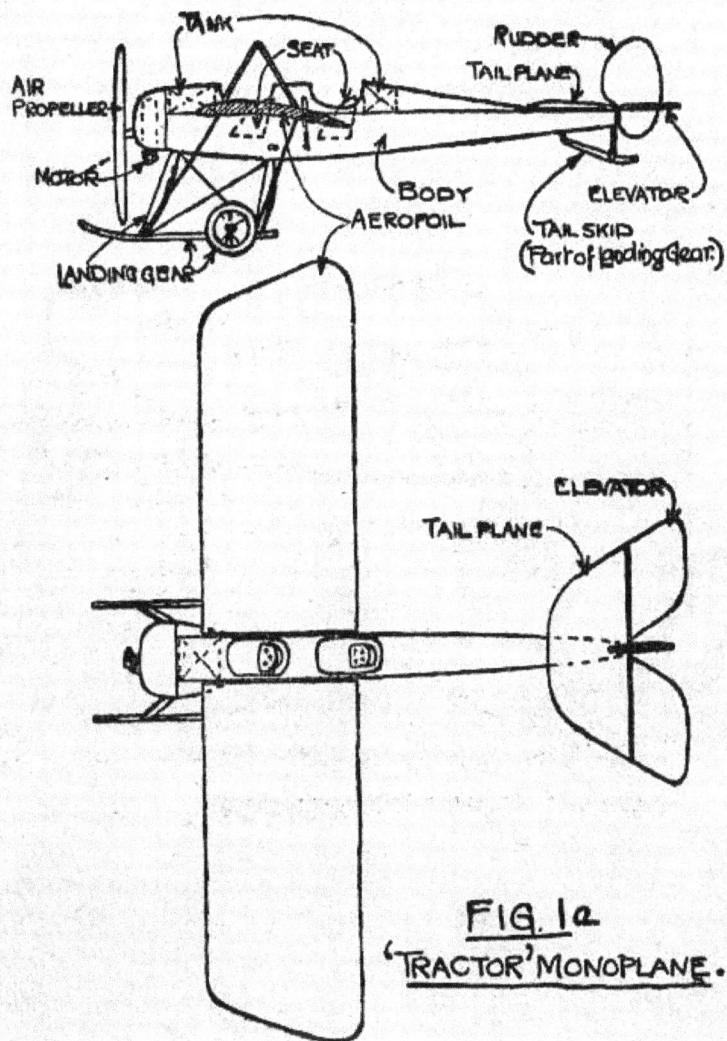

FIG. 1a
'TRACTOR' MONOPLANE.

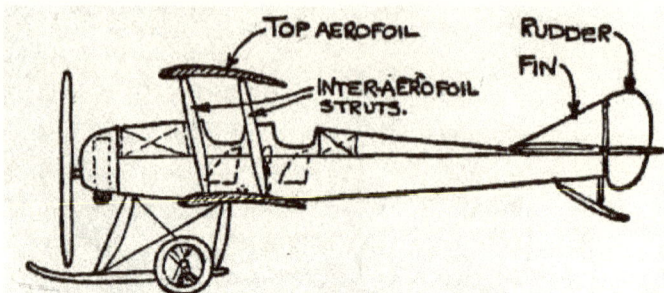

FIG. 2a.

'TRACTOR' BIPLANE.

Top Plan approximately same as for Tractor Monoplane.

as possible through the C.G., or slightly below it, and head-resistance kept above thrust; but in neither case should the divergence be great.

It is necessary now to consider these four forces in more detail. The total weight, W_T, for any particular machine is a constant—at least, we may consider it so, since in preliminary design one always considers the machine as fully loaded. The total lift, L_T, is the sum of several forces which all vary according to the attitude of the machine to its flight-path, and which also all vary approximately as the square of the speed. We shall consider it as made up of lift of aerofoils L_A, vertical reaction on body of machine 1_B, and vertical reaction on tail of machine 1_T. I call it "lift," for aerofoils only, for it may be a downward force on one or other, or both, of the other members.

The thrust of the air propeller, T, depends upon the power given to it, upon its efficiency E, upon its revolutions per second r, and upon the speed along the flight-path v. It is matter for discussion later.

The total head-resistance, R_T, we shall consider as the sum of the horizontal reactions upon the aerofoils (which we shall call henceforth "dynamic resistance" or "drift," and denote by R_A), upon the body r_B, upon the landing gear r_G, upon the tail r_T. We shall henceforth call total head-resistance minus "dynamic head-resistance," "residual head-resistance," and denote it by R_r.

Having noted what kind of machine we have to design and the elementary conditions necessary for it to fly in a straight line; I had better turn next to the consideration of our sources of data, for designing the various members of the machine.

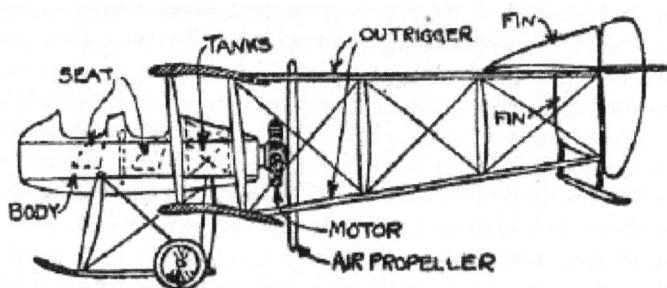

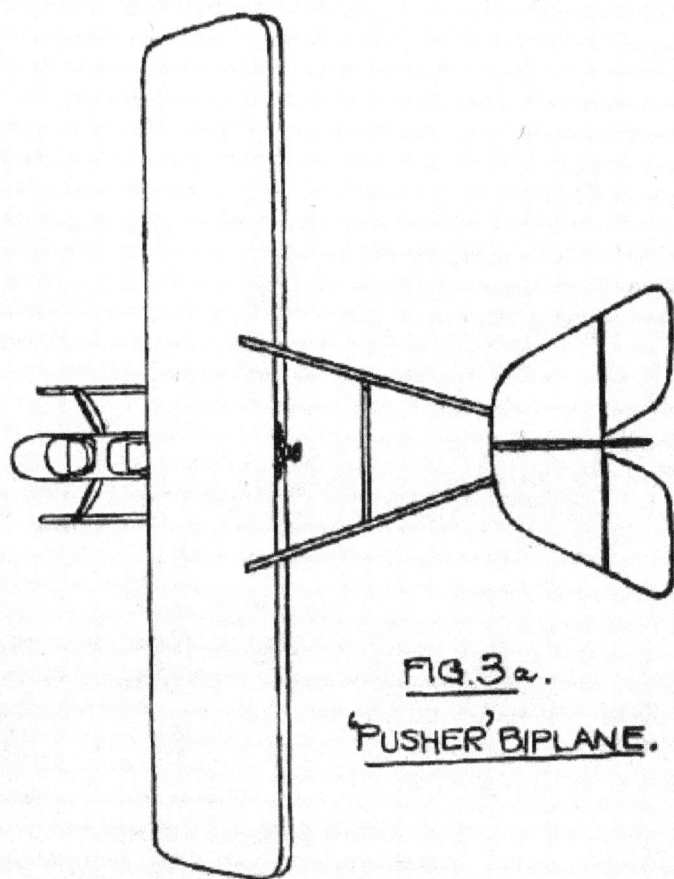

SEAT

TANKS

OUTRIGGER

FIN

FIN

BODY

MOTOR

AIR PROPELLER

FIG. 3 a.

'PUSHER' BIPLANE.

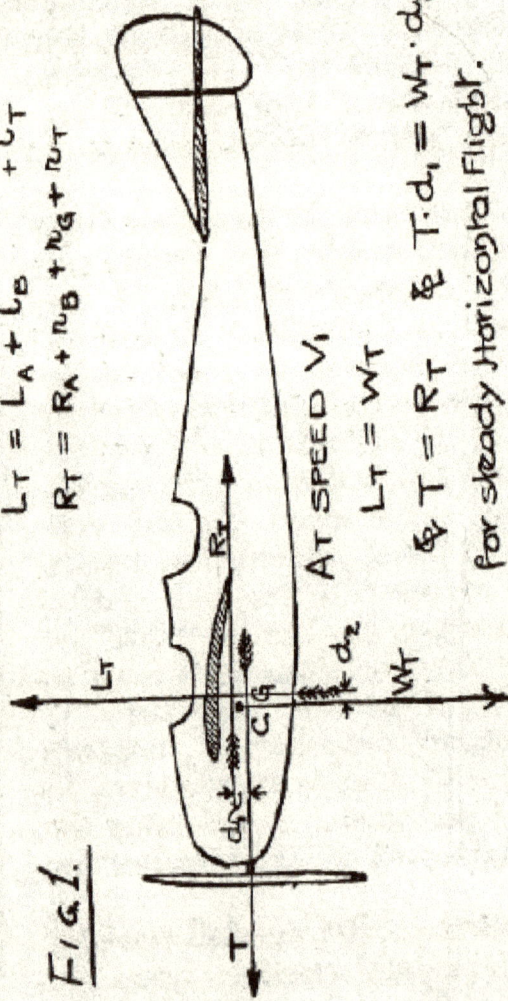

Fig. 1.

$$L_T = L_A + L_B + L_T$$

$$R_T = R_A + r_B + r_G + r_T$$

At speed V,

$$L_T = W_T$$

$$\&\ T = R_T \quad \& \quad T \cdot d_1 = W_T \cdot d_2$$

for steady Horizontal Flight.

L_T = Total Lift.
L_A = Lift of Aerofoils.
L_B = Vertical reaction on Body.

L_T = " " " Tail.

R_T = Total Resistance.

r_A = Horizontal Reaction on Aerofoils, or 'Drift', or 'Dynamic Resistance'.

r_B = Horizontal reaction on Body.
r_G = " " " " Landing Gear.
r_T = " " " " Tail.

$R_T - R_A$ = 'Residual Resistance' R_r

Motors.

The motor is the most expensive, the most important, and the heaviest single item, and it must be properly mounted, cooled and fed.

It is useful and convenient to prepare a table of motors, as shown in Fig. 2. In the first column we have name and type of motor; in the second normal full b.h.p.; in the third, r.p.s. of motor at this power; in the fourth, weight of motor in lbs. complete with carburettor, magneto, piping, etc., also radiator and water (if water cooled); in the fifth, petrol consumption in galls./hour at full normal power; in the sixth, the same for lubricant; in the seventh, weight of suitable mounting and suitable shields or "cowling"; in the eighth, weight of suitable air propeller with coupling; in the ninth, tenth, eleventh, twelfth and thirteenth columns we have total weight of motor (complete as in col. 4) with mounting, cowling, propeller, petrol, lubricant and tanks, for 2, 4, 6, 8 and 10 hours running respectively, at full normal power.

As to how the figures in this table are obtained. Weight of motor complete is given us by the makers, likewise the power, revs., and petrol and oil consumption. The weight of a suitable mounting is a matter of deduction from the actual weights of satisfactory mountings for known cases. I have assumed that weight of mounting varies directly as weight of motor, and have taken it as 1-7th weight of motor for a rotary, and 1-10th weight of motor for a stationary engine.

The weight of "cowling" I have taken as varying as the square root of the weight of the motor, and as equal to twice square root of weight of motor for a rotary, and one-half this weight for a stationary motor.

The weight of tanks I have taken as varying directly as the capacity, and as 1-5th of the weight of the contents (when full, of course), taking petrol as 7.2 lbs. per gallon, and lubricating oil at 10 lbs. per gallon.

The weight of propeller I have taken as varying as the square root of the horse-power and as numerically equal to three times square root horse-power in lbs.

All these weights are fair ones from such data as I have come across. You will understand that they are only approximate, but they are accurate enough for first estimate of weights, and probably err on the safe, that is, the heavy, side.

From this table, then, we can obtain the total weight of power plant for a considerable number of different powers and for any length of maximum power running between the extreme limits of present requirements.

133

(1) NAME & TYPE OF MOTOR	(2) Full Normal BHP	(3) r.u.p.s at Full Normal BHP	(4) Weight of Motor Complete	(5) Petrol Cons Galls/Hour	(6) Oil Cons/Hour	(7) Wgt of Mtg etc	(8) Wgt of Propeller	(9) W 2 Hours	(10) W 4 Hours	(11) W 6 Hours	(12) W 8 Hours	(13) W 10 Hours
50HP GNOME Rotary AC	38	20	170	5.0	1.0	50	19	349	459	569	679	789
80HP Gnome Rotary A.C.	68	20	210	7.5	1.7	59	25	464	634	804	974	1144
100HP Gnome Rotary Ac	95	20	320	10	2	82	29	651	871	1091	1311	1531
80HP le Rhone Rotary AC	85	20	250	8.5	1.8	68	28	536	726	916	1106	1296
70HP Renault Stationary AC	72	30	350	7.0	1.0	54	26	574	718	862	1006	1150
120HP Austin Daimler Stationary WC	125	20	600	9.5	.6	80	34	892	1070	1248	1426	1604
90HP Canton Unné Stationary WC	85	21	450	7.5	.6	66	28	688	832	976	1120	1264
200HP Canton Unné Stationary WC	200	21	900	16	1.0	120	42	1362	1662	1962	2262	2562

TABLE FOR MOTOR WEIGHTS.

wgt (7) = $\frac{1}{2}$(2) + 2√(2) in lbs, for Rotary

= $\frac{1}{10}$(2) + √(2) for Stationary.

wgt (8) = 3√BHP in lbs
wgt Tanks = $\frac{1}{3}$ wgt contents full.
Petrol = 7.2 lbs/gall.
Oil = 10 lbs/gall.

FIG. 2.

We must now consider what results we can get from aerofoils and how to estimate the weights of the other members of the machine before we can decide upon what motor to employ and commence the actual design.

Data for aerofoils are founded entirely upon experimental work. I do not think it is possible to calculate from first principles the re-actions upon a body, of any but the simplest forms, in an air current, though, of course, we can obtain by interpolation and analysis many further figures from experimentally determined bases. The method almost universally employed is that of suspending a model in a steady air current of known direction and velocity, and measuring the re-actions and moments upon it by means of a suitable balance.

Let us, then, consider an aerofoil moving at a uniform velocity in still air, or, what is equivalent as regards the air reactions upon it, stationary in a steady air current. (Fig. 3)

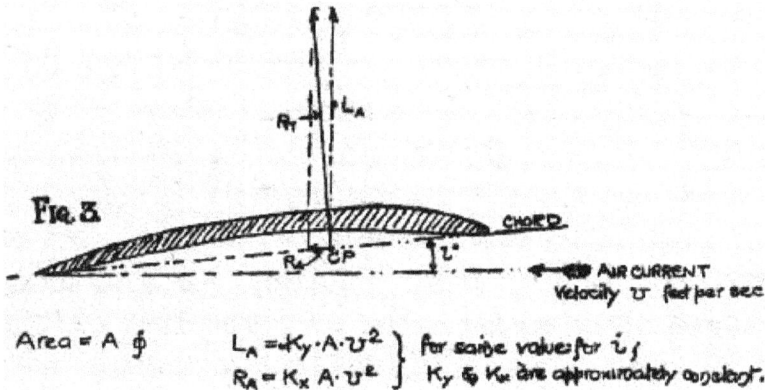

Fig. 3.

Area = A ⌀

$$L_A = K_y \cdot A \cdot v^2$$
$$R_A = K_x \cdot A \cdot v^2$$
for same value for i;
K_y & K_x are approximately constant.

Let us denote the area in square feet by A, the angle in degrees of the chord of the wing section to the relative air current by i, and the relative air velocity in feet per sec. by v. There is, of course, a total resultant re-action RT upon this aerofoil, which it is most convenient to measure, and consider as the sum of two reactions, one LA vertical to the direction of the air current, our "lift," the other RA along the air current, our "dynamic resistance" or "drift." For convenience in varying A and v these forces are usually tabulated for different values of i in the form of coefficients. We can write:

Lift, L_A - Ky Av^2 in lbs. weight.

Drift, R_A - Kx Av^2 in lbs. weight,

for these coefficients of lift and drift, Ky and Kx, are approximately

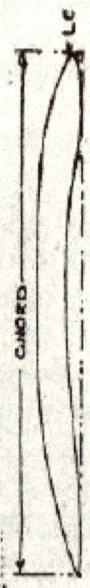

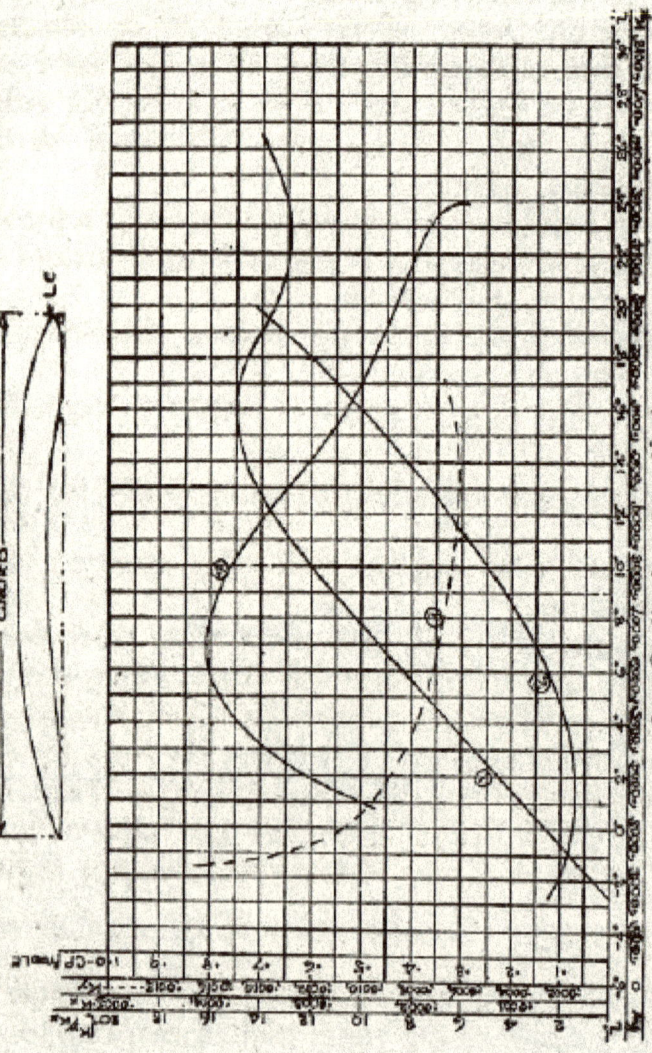

FIG. 4

constant for similar aerofoils and for the same value of i for all values of A and of v.

Our data for aerofoils, then, is based upon experimentally determined values at different values of i, for the coefficients Ky and Kx, and for the position of "centre of pressure," or intersection of line of total resultant re-action with the chord, for model size aerofoils.

It is useful to tabulate the dynamic properties of aerofoils in the following manner:—For every model for which we can get reliable data we should make on tracing cloth a standard sheet. (Fig. 4). On each of these sheets, and in the same position, we draw an accurate scale section of its aerofoil with a standard chord length of, say, 10".

On each sheet, and in the same position, we also draw a standard squared table for its respective curves of Ky, Kx and of locus of centre of pressure, with a base of value for i (say, ½" representing 1° of i), and with ordinate values for both Ky and Kx (say, ½" representing .0001 of Ky value, and 2" representing .0001 of Kx value). The abscissae values should range from—6° to + 30° for i, and the ordinate values from o to .002 of Ky value. That is to say, our standard table will be 18" long and 10" high.

On this table 1" of ordinate value will represent a distance of centre of pressure from leading edge of aerofoil of .1 of chord.

On this same table we draw a fourth curve Ky over Kx (i.e. Lift over Drift) value on a base of Ky value; ½" of ordinate value representing unity for Lift over Drift value, and 1" of abscissa value representing .0001 of Ky value.

We can now, by superimposing the sheets, compare any of our aerofoil forms. The sections and tables will lie one over the other, and we can see which form gives us the best Ky (or Lift Coefficient) value at any value of i, the lowest Kx (or Drift Coefficient) value at any value of i, the least travel of centre of pressure, and the highest value for Lift over Drift for any value of lift coefficient.

We must note here that these tables should all be for models of the same plan form, i.e., of the same ratio of Span over Chord (or "Aspect Ratio") and of the same form of ends. The National Physical Laboratory generally employs a standard rectangular plan form of 18" span and 3" chord, i.e., of Aspect Ratio 6. The coefficient values should also (for absolutely safe comparison) be for the same size of model at the same air speed.

I remarked before that these coefficients were constants (for the same value of i) for varying values of both A and V. I must now, in somewhat Hibernian vein, remark that these "constants" are not quite constant. The Ky, or lift coefficient, has been found by experiment to be fairly constant for widely varying values of A and V. We shall consider it as such, and directly use model Ky values for our calculations for full-sized machines, noting that any error will probably be to the good. But the Kx, or drift coefficient, decreases slightly as A increases, and also decreases considerably as V increases. This has the meaning that the drift coefficient of our full-size aerofoil will be less than that of the model, but it also means that we cannot determine quite so accurately as we should like to, what it will be for our full-size aerofoil, especially if it be for a fast machine.

It is most probable that this difference is due to that part of the total re-action caused by skin-friction, the component of which is small in the direction of lift but large in the direction of drift; and skin-friction coefficient we know to increase both with increase of A and with increase of V^2. The best thing that we can do is to use the results which the N.P.L. gives us in the latest report of the Advisory Committee. (See Fig. 5).

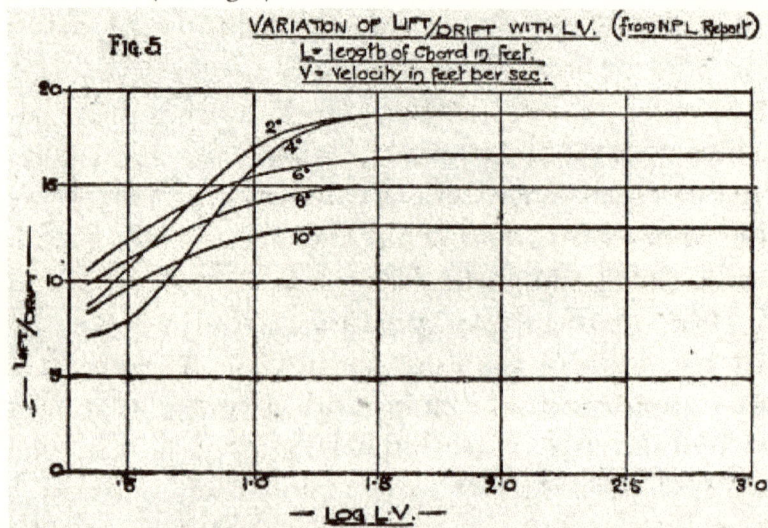

Fig. 5.

VARIATION OF LIFT/DRIFT WITH LV. (from NPL Report)
L = length of Chord in feet.
V = Velocity in feet per sec.

(Fig. 5.) Here we have, for several different i values, curves of lift/drift on a base of log LV, where L = length of chord in feet, and V = velocity in feet per second. By using this we can from model figures obtain fairly accurately those for a full size aerofoil at any speed.

It is necessary now to consider the effect of plan form. (Fig. 6.) Assuming first that the plan form of our aerofoils is rectangular and that

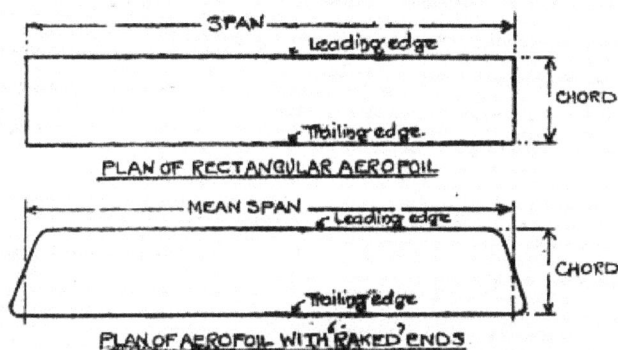

PLAN OF RECTANGULAR AEROFOIL

PLAN OF AEROFOIL WITH 'RAKED' ENDS

$$\text{ASPECT RATIO} = \frac{\text{SPAN}}{\text{CHORD}}$$

FIG. 6.

TABLE FOR VARIATION OF ASPECT RATIO. (N.P.L.)

Value of $i°$	ASPECT RATIO											
	8/1		7/1		6/1		5/1		4/1		3/1	
	Ky	L/D	Ky	L/D	Ky	L/D	Ky	L/D	Ky	L/D	Ky	L/D
-2	·028	1·0	·012	·4	·044	1·8	·052	2·4	·055	2·4	·055	2·3
0	·128	6·1	·117	5·2	·109	5·2	·110	5·5	·141	6·7	·112	5·0
2	·222	11·1	·219	11·2	·212	10·7	·199	10·2	·214	9·5	·173	7·7
4	·298	14·2	·300	14·6	·289	13·8	·283	12·6	·289	11·4	·246	9·6
6	·398	15·5	·366	14·9	·372	13·4	·354	12·5	·345	11·1	·320	10·1
8	·487	14·6	·447	13·5	·469	12·7	·430	11·4	·423	10·4	·389	9·3
10	·560	13·3	·516	12·7	·536	11·5	·579	10·5	·485	9·6	·445	9·0
12	·636	12·2	·598	11·6	·612	10·7	·595	10·1	·546	8·6	·516	7·9
14	·686	10·9	·670	10·3	·686	9·9	·656	9·2	·609	8·3	·566	8·1
16	·685	8·2	·680	8·5	·686	8·3	·685	8·2	·673	7·1	·619	6·4
18	·673	5·6	·689	5·4	·686	5·7	·663	5·8	·683	5·8	·665	5·8
20	·653	3·9	·660	4·0	·662	3·9	·645	3·8	·643	3·7	·667	4·4

Ky values in above Table are in 'Absolute' units: to convert to lb. foot, sec., units multiply above values by ·00236 we vary the Aspect Ratio only:

The National Physical Laboratory gives us this table of Lift Coefficient values, and Lift to Drift values for an aerofoil of constant section and of Aspect Ratio varying from 3 to 1 to 8 to 1 at values of i from— 2° to + 20°. I suggest using this table comparatively; *i.e.*, suppose we have figures for a model of 6 to 1 Aspect Ratio and wish to calculate its properties for some other Aspect Ratio, say, 4 to 1. We shall take it that its values at 4 to 1 will be to its relative values at 6 to 1 as are the corresponding values in this table for 6 to 1 to those for 4 to 1.

It appears, from such few experiments as have been made, that it slightly increases an aerofoil's efficiency to rake the ends somewhat, making the trailing edge longer than the leading edge. This is because such a formation of ends decreases the end losses. And probably the lower the Aspect Ratio the more should the ends rake. In practice, however, it is better not to rake the ends too much, as we cannot then get the best distribution of stay attachments along both front and rear spars.

I suggest about 30° Rake for 4 to Aspect Ratio, 25° for 5 to 1, and 20° for 6 to 1, but these are quite arbitrary values.

From a strength point of view, it is advantageous to taper the aerofoils from root to tip. But as this means a structure considerably more difficult and costly to make, I do not think it is quite justified.

As regards choice of Aspect Ratio:—For the same surface, the lower the Aspect Ratio the stronger is the aerofoil, or the lighter for the same strength, but the lower will be the maximum Lift to Drift value and the maximum value for Lift. The efficiency at very small and very large values for i is not much affected, and, in fact, appears from this table to be rather better for the lower Aspect Ratios. We must bear in mind that a low Aspect Ratio is worse for both lateral and directional stability than a high one. Taking everything into consideration, I would suggest 5 to 1 Aspect Ratio for monoplanes and small biplanes, and 6 to 1 to 7 to 1 for large biplanes.

Next, for biplanes only of course, to consider the effect of gap and stagger. Fig. 7. From model experiments, we find that the greater the gap the higher the efficiency, whilst stagger also increases the efficiency somewhat. The gap amount, however, introduces the question of weight and head resistance of struts and stays, the greater the gap the greater these become. So, we must compromise, and I should suggest a gap of .8 of Chord up to equal to Chord, the smaller value for fast and relatively high-powered machines, the larger for slower and

140

Fig. 7.

GAP, 'STAGGER', CHORD, CHORD

Figs for Gap

C'_B	Ratio GAP/CHORD	C_B
·81	·4	·62
·82	·8	·77
·84	1·0	·82
·85	1·2	·86
·89	1·6	·89

C_B is multiplying factor to obtain Biplane Lift Coeff.¹ˢ from Monoplane figures. C'_B is ditto for values for ½b.

Figs for Stagger

For stagger = ·44 Gap both Lift Coefficient & Lift/Drift value improved by about 5%.

less highly powered ones.

The increase in efficiency is not very great in a staggered disposition, and it increases structural difficulties, especially if the means for obtaining lateral control is by warping the aerofoils. Stagger may, however, be of considerable value for improving the view obtainable downwards from the machine. Hence, I should suggest that the question of stagger should mainly depend upon the disposition of the pilot and passenger in the machine, noting that if we use a heavy stagger, we should use ailerons and not warp.

We have then data for the dynamic properties of model aerofoils and know how we can use them for calculations on full-size ones.

Let us turn to the consideration of the weight of aerofoils as a structure, for, unfortunately, they have got to lift their own weight first and then supply their surplus energy to lifting the rest of the machine.

(Fig. 8.) Similar structures will bear the same ultimate load per unit area, which means in our case that similar aerofoils will have the same "factor of safety" for the same value of *useful* loading in lbs. per square foot.

Taking basic figures from actual satisfactory aerofoils, we shall assume that we can construct an aerofoil of 100 sq. ft. surface, to weigh 70 lbs., and to stand 5.7 lbs. per sq. ft. total loading with the margin of strength necessary. This figure for weight, *i.e.*, .7 lbs. per sq. ft., includes the weights of stays for a monoplane and of stays and struts for a biplane. Now we consider the aerofoil as stressed only by the useful

WEIGHT OF AEROFOILS.

For Similar Aerofoils:— FIG. 8.

Let w = wgt in lbs/ ф

 A = Area in ф & L = length of Chord in feet

Then wA = weight of aerofoil $\propto L^3$

$$\frac{W_T}{A} \cdot \frac{Total\ weight\ of\ Machine}{Area\ of\ aerofoils} = Mean\ Total\ Loading\ in\ lbs/ф.$$

So $\frac{W_T}{A} - w$ = Useful loading in lbs/ф & = load for Stress

If $\frac{W_T}{A} - w$ = constant then for same strength

$$wA \propto L^3 \quad \text{or} \quad w \propto L \quad \text{or} \quad w \propto \sqrt{A} \quad (I)$$
$$\text{or} \quad w = k_1 \sqrt{A}$$

for aerofoils of same strength & same Area

$$k_1 \propto \frac{W_T}{A} - w \quad \cdots (ii)$$

From previous Data

If $\frac{W_T}{A} - w$ = 5 lbs/ф then k_1 = .07

Hence, from (ii), — k_1 = .014 $\left(\frac{W_T}{A} - w\right)$

& hence, from (i), — w = .014 $\left(\frac{W_T}{A} - w\right)\sqrt{A}$ lbs/ф

Equation for wgt of Aerofoils

loading, *i.e.*, total load, WT, minus aerofoil weight, since in flight it is stressed only by the lift it exerts over and above its own weight. We shall take it then that since the weight of similar aerofoils varies as the cube of the linear dimension and the surface as the square, the weight per sq. ft., w, will vary as the square root of the total surface, A, for the same unital useful loading, or value of WT over A - w.

Further, we shall take it that for aerofoils of the same total area, within the limits of useful loading desirable to employ, the weight per sq. ft., w, varies directly as the unital useful loading WT over A - w, for the same strength.

We see that on these assumptions for a total surface of 100 sq. ft. the weight per sq. foot will be .7 lbs. for 5 lbs. per sq. ft. useful loading, but for a total surface of 400 sq. ft. it will be 1.4 lbs. for the same useful-loading. This is one of the basic facts against the building of large sized machines; for unless we can improve our structure (and of course

142

the larger the machine the better chance we have of so doing) the greater must the proportion of aerofoil weight to useful load become.

We have then, that since

$$w = k_1 \sqrt{A} \text{ lbs. per sq. ft., and}$$

$$k_1 = .07 \text{ when } \frac{W_T}{A} - w = 5.0 \text{ lbs. per sq. ft., and}$$

$$k \propto \frac{W_T}{A} - w \text{ (useful loading)}$$

therefore $k_1 = .014 \left(\dfrac{W_T}{A} - w \right)$

and therefore

$$w = .014 \sqrt{A} \left(\frac{W_T}{A} - w \right) \text{ in lbs. per sq. ft.,}$$

an equation for the weight per sq. ft. of our aerofoils, in terms of total aerofoil area and total weight of aeroplane.

ITEM WEIGHTS

We must now get figures for our other weights. (Fig. 9.)

Generally speaking, the size of the Tail, Rudder, and Vertical Fin (if used) will vary directly as the size of the Wings (this assumes, of course, approximately constant proportions for the machine). I suggest, then, taking the necessary weight of Tail and Rudder and Fin as a proportion of the aerofoil total weight, and a fair figure to take is one-fifth.

The weight of the body introduces the question of the number of people the machine is to carry. A sufficiently strong body of the timber and wire, fabric covered, girder type can be made, of about 20 ft. length and 2 ft. mean breadth and depth, to weigh about 90 lbs., *i.e.* if $l = 20$ feet, b and d = 2 feet then $W_B = 90$ lbs.

Since in such a structure the struts are (generally speaking), very strong compared to the fore and aft members, for the kind of stresses to which it is subjected, we shall assume that the weight will vary directly as the breadth and depth, but as the square of the length. Hence, we get an equation for weight of Body $W_B = .057\, l^2\, b\, d$ in lbs.

As for the contents of this body. We can seat each person properly for about 10 lbs., and the weight of control mechanism will be from 30 lbs. to 50 lbs., dependent upon the type employed.

ITEM WEIGHTS. Fig. 9

(i) Weight of Tail unit, i.e. of Tail Plane, Elevators, Rudder & Fin (if used)

$$W_T = \tfrac{1}{5} \text{ total Aerofoil wgt} = \tfrac{1}{5} W \cdot A$$

(ii) Weight of Body, W_B —

If l, b & d represent respectively length, mean breadth & mean depth of Body in feet

$$\text{then } W_B \propto l^2 \cdot b \cdot d$$

+ If $l = 20 ft$, $b = 2 ft$, $d = 2 ft$ then $W_B = 90$ lbs

$$\text{Hence } W_B = \cdot 057 \, l^2 \cdot b \cdot d \text{ in lbs}$$

(iii) Weight of Seating $= 10$ lbs per person

(iv) Weight of Controls $= 30 - 50$ lbs, dependent on type.

(v) Weight of landing gear complete, W_g —

$$W_g = \tfrac{1}{14} W_T, \text{ of this wgt. of Tail Skid} = \tfrac{W_g}{20}$$

It remains only to consider the weight of suitable landing gear. I think it fair to consider the weight of the Landing Gear, W_G, as varying directly as the total loaded weight, W_T, of the machine, and I think a suitable one can be designed at one-fourteenth of the total loaded weight This weight we shall take as including the weight, of the Tail Skid. For an average landing gear and tail skid we may consider weight of Tail Skid alone as = 1/20 of total weight of Landing Gear.

First Estimates.

We are now in a position, having been given certain requirements, to make a first estimate of weights, deciding in so doing upon the motor to employ.

The designer is generally required to produce a machine to carry a certain number of people, petrol and oil for so many hours' flight at full power, a certain weight of observing instruments, perhaps some weapons of offence, fully loaded to be able to fly at not less than a certain maximum, and not more than a certain minimum speed, and to climb at not less than a certain minimum rate.

Probably the simplest course to take in this brief outline of designing methods is to assume a certain set of conditions has been given and see how we should set about trying to fulfil it. We shall assume, therefore, that we are asked to design a machine to carry two people, pilot and passenger, to fly at 80 m.p.h. maximum and 40 m.p.h. minimum, to climb at 7 feet per second fully loaded, to carry petrol and oil for 4 hours, to have a good range of view downwards for the passenger, to carry a full outfit of instruments, *i.e.*, barograph, compass, map case, watches, engines, revolution counter, air speed indicator, inclinometers, etc.

We must, of course, keep everything as small, compact and simple as possible to maintain strength and avoid weight.

To keep the fuselage weight and head resistance as low as possible we shall make it a tandem-seated machine.

As a good downward view is required for the observer, we shall seat him in front of the pilot as far forward as possible.

As the machine must necessarily be of a fair total weight and of fairly light loading to fly at the necessary minimum speed, we shall make it a biplane.

Further, we shall give it sufficient stagger for the observer to be able to see vertically, or nearly vertically, down over the leading edge of the lower aerofoils.

This will probably mean a rather large stagger, so we shall decide on ailerons for lateral control, these having the further advantage over warping that they give much better control power at low speeds (which entails, of course, large values of i). Warping is equivalent to increasing the i value of one aerofoil tip; at slow speeds this may mean *no* increased lift, as the machine may already be flying with its aerofoils at their attitude for maximum lift, but it *will* mean increased drift with tendency to spin in the wrong direction. But pulling down an aileron is equivalent to increasing the camber of part of the aerofoil, and, hence, will give increased lift at any value for i.

We shall make the Body 20 feet long by 2 feet mean depth and breadth, and, therefore, of 90 lbs. weight, the weight decided on before for this particular size.

We must allow 350 lbs. for pilot and passenger in their flying kit, and 20 lbs, for seating them.

The controls, being not dual and being for ailerons, we shall take at the lightest weight, 30 lbs.

For the full kit of instruments called for we must allow 30 lbs.

This gives us a total weight of Body and contents of 510 lbs.

We now come to rather an *impasse*, as we cannot get weights of

Aerofoils, Tail Unit and Landing Gear until we have fixed on the engine, and we should like to know the total weight in order to fix on the engine. So, we must make a first choice of an engine, judging from some previous machine.

We know that with the 80 Gnome one can make a tractor biplane to fly at 40 to 78 m.p.h. with 4 hours' fuel and oil, pilot and passenger, and climb at about the rate we require. We shall, therefore, need more power than the 80 Gnome for our machine; but, of course, we want to use as low a power as possible.

Let us try the 80-p.h. Le Rhone. From our weight table for engines, we find that total weight for this motor with 4 hours' petrol and oil, tanks, mounting, cowling and propeller will be 726 lbs.

We now have total weight less Aerofoils, Tail Unit and Landing Gear = 1,246 lbs. There remains to fix on wing form and loading, and thence Wing, Tail Unit, and Landing Gear weights.

The total weight WT will be equal to 1,246 lbs. + WG + (W x A) + (1/5 W x A) (Fig. 10), where WG = weight of Landing Gear, including Tail Skid, W = weight of Aerofoils in lbs, per square foot, and A = total surface of Aerofoils in square feet. The 1/5 WA is, of course, the Tail unit weight.

Further we have that WG = 1/14 WT—
Hence, 13/1 WT = 1246 + 1.2 WA. (1)

CHOICE OF AEROFOIL

We must now fix upon what form of aerofoil to employ and what loading.

The first thing to note is that the machine has to be able to fly at 40 m.p.h., or about 59 f.p.s. So, the maximum Ky value for the aerofoils must be such as to give us lift per square foot at 58 feet per second equal to the total loading per square foot that we shall choose.

This may seem a small margin to allow for obtaining the slow speed, but it must be remembered, that at the slow speed, and consequent cabre, or tail-down, attitude of the machine, there will be a certain amount of added lift from the tail and body of the machine, and a slight upward component of propeller pull.

Also, we must cut the slow speed as fine as possible to get the greatest possible high speed.

Now, for 4 lbs. per square foot, total loading at 58 feet per second maximum Ky must be = .00119

For 4½ lbs. max. Ky must be = .00134.

ESTIMATE FOR TOTAL WEIGHT ETC.   **FIG. 10**

Total weight $W_T = 1246 + W_G + WA + \frac{1}{5} WA$ (lbs)

Whence — $\frac{13}{14} W_T = 1246 + 1\cdot2\, WA$ (lbs) (i)

Taking $U_{(min)} = 58\,$ fps —

For $\frac{W_T}{A} = 4$ lbs/ϕ	$K_{y(max)} = \cdot00119$		
" " 4·5 "	" $\cdot00134$	For Biplane
" " 5·0 "	" $\cdot00149$	
" " 5·5 "	" $\cdot00164$	

Taking $U_{(max)} = 120$ fps

$$\frac{K_y \text{ for } 120\,\text{fps}}{K_y \text{ for } 58\,\text{fps}} = \frac{58^2}{120^2} = \cdot 233$$

Taking K_y biplane with Gap = to Chord & Stagger = ·4 Chord

K_y Biplane = ·85 K_y Monoplane

Hence necessary Model Monoplane Figs —

For $\frac{W_T}{A} = 4$ lbs/ϕ K_y at 58 fps = ·00140

" " " 4·5 " "   " " " " = ·00158

" " " 5·0 " "   " " " " = ·00176

" " " 5·5 " "   " " " " = ·00193

K_y for 120 fps = ·233 of above values

If K_y max = ·0015   loading = 4·3 lbs/ϕ at 58 fps

If $W_T = 1900$ lbs & $\frac{W_T}{A} = 4·3$ lb/ϕ then $A = 440\,\phi$

From Equation $W = ·014\sqrt{A}\left(\frac{W_T}{A} - W\right)$

$W = ·014\sqrt{440}\,(4·3 - W)$

or $W = ·98$ lbs/ϕ

& $WA = \underline{430\,\text{lbs}}$ (ii)

Hence from (i) & (ii)

$\frac{13}{14} W_T = 1246 + (1·2 \times 430)$ or $W_T = 1900$ lbs

For 5 lbs. max. Ky must be = .00149.

For 5½ lbs. max. Ky must be = .00164.

All these being values for a biplane, of course.

We must now consider our high-speed:

The high speed is to be 80 m.p.h., or 117 feet per second. Considering it as 120 feet per second we see, of course, that the Ky values for this speed must be 58^2 over 120^2 of the Ky values for 58 feet per second, as loading is constant. That is to say:

Ky at 120 f.p.s. must = .233 Ky at 58 f.p.s.

Corresponding Monoplane Values

We must next, as our machine is a biplane, and our figures for model aerofoils are for single or monoplane form, obtain from our tables for effects of gap and stagger the necessary corresponding monoplane Ky values. We shall assume that we shall make gap = chord and stagger = about .4 of chord. We shall, therefore, as sufficiently accurate for the present, take that Ky biplane = .85 Ky monoplane, as it would be about .82 for this gap and no stagger, and we obtain about 4 *per cent*, increase of efficiency due to the stagger.

That is to say, the necessary biplane Kys we have found for different loadings, must be multiplied by 1.18 for monoplane tests. We get then:

For—

4.0 lbs. per sq. ft. loading Ky max. must be			.00140
4.5 " " "			.00158
5.0 " " "			.00176
5.5 " " "			.00193

and Ky high-speed = .233 of these values as we saw before.

We turn now to our data sheets for Model Monoplane Aerofoils and fix upon the best form for our case.

We have to pick out that Aerofoil which, having a maximum Ky of .00140 or over, will give us the highest value for Lift to Drift for a Ky value = .233 of its maximum value; that is, we must consult the curve of Ky value, and the curve of Lift to Drift on a base of Ky value, for all our data sheets, and pick out the best Aerofoil for this case.

We shall assume that we have done this, and have found the best Aerofoil form for us to be one which for a maximum Ky of .0015 gives us, at Ky = .233 of .0015 (or .00035), a Lift to Drift of 10/1,

With this Aerofoil we must have a loading of 4.3 lbs. per square foot.

We must now make a shot at the total weight WT, as we shall then be able to get a figure for total Aerofoil Area, thence for Aerofoil weight, thence a figure for total weight, which must be very nearly the same as our guessed weight, or we must guess again with increased wisdom.

We shall guess, then, that the machine is going to weigh, fully loaded, 1,900 lbs., and it will, therefore, need $\dfrac{1900}{4.3}$, or 440 square feet of Aerofoil surface at the 4.3 lbs. per square foot total loading.

From our previously determined equation :

$$ w = .014 \sqrt{A} \left(\frac{W^T}{A} - w \right) $$

We get that $w = .014 \sqrt{440} \,(4.3 - w)$
whence $w = .98$ lbs. per sq. ft.
This, then, gives us Aerofoil weight $= 430$ lbs., and we get that $\dfrac{13}{14}$ WT $= 1762$, or WT $= 1900$ lbs.; of this, Tail unit weight is 86 lbs., Landing Gear weight $= 136$ lbs., and of this, again, 7 lbs. is Tail Skid.

This is our guessed weight (I admit that I guessed once or twice in getting out these figures, but have spared you the tedium by quoting the right guess at once); so, we can take the figures for total weight and wing surface as found.

Definite Design.

We have now fixed weights, surface, aerofoil form and motor, and can proceed with the design.

We shall, as this is a largish machine, choose an aspect ratio of 6 to 1, which gives us 4 aerofoils of 6.15 feet chord by 17.5 feet "mean" span, which with the top centre plane of 2 feet span, gives us a total "mean" span of 37.0 feet, and our total surface (which is surface of 4 aerofoils + top centre plane), of 440 square feet. I talk of "mean" span, as we shall employ ends raking at 20° for our aerofoils.

We must now draw out a side elevation of the body of the machine with seats, tanks, motor, and tail skid, keeping all the weights as close together as possible. (Fig. 11). We shall employ a "non-lifting" Tail plane, that is to say, a form symmetrical about its central horizontal plane and with this plane parallel to the axis of the propeller.

This form is perhaps the safest to employ, as it will give no difference in lift or depression, whether in the propeller slip stream (when the motor is running) or not (when the motor is stopped). We shall set the chord of the aerofoils at 3° to the propeller axis.

We now require to place our Aerofoils and Landing Gear, less Tail Skid, of course, on the body in such a manner that the total reaction on the Aerofoils, at 3° value for i, passes through the CG of the whole machine (of this more *anon*), and that the centre of the wheel axle of the Landing Gear is about 12" ahead of it.

FIG. 11.

ITEM	W	L	h	W×L(+)	W×L(-)	W×h(+)	W×h(-)
Propeller	28	+2·0	-	56	-	-	-
Motor	250	+·7	-	175	-	-	-
Cowling	32	+·4	+·4	13	-	13	-
Motor Mounting	36	-·2	-	-	7	-	-
Oil & Tank	86	-·6	+1·3	-	52	112	-
Passenger	175	-2·5	+1·0	-	390	175	-
Passengers Seat	10	-2·8	+·4	-	28	4	-
Petrol & Tank	294	-5·2	+1·4	-	1530	412	-
Body	90	-6·7	-	-	602	-	-
Instruments	30	-7·1	+1·5	-	213	45	-
Controls	90	-7·5	-	-	225	-	-
Pilot	175	-8·7	+1·0	-	1520	175	-
Pilots Seat	10	-9·1	+·4	-	91	4	-
Tail	86	-19·0	+1·0	-	1630	86	-
Tail Skid	7	-19·7	-1·0	-	138	-	7
Aerofoils complete	430	-4·9	+2·8	-	2107	1208	-
Landing Gear	129	-2·5	-3·9	-	322	-	503
TOTAL (loaded)	1898	4·55	+·91	244	8855	2234	510

W = wgt of Item in lbs.
L = Normal dist of CG of Item from line Y-Y. +ahead, -behind.
h = " " " " " " " " X-X + above, -below

150

This, of course, is another trial and error process, and had best be arrived at as follows:—Draw on a piece of tracing paper the side elevation of the Aerofoils (to same scale as Body, of course), with correct gap and stagger, also a base line AB inclined at 3° to the chords. From model figures for the Aerofoil form mark on chord of each Aerofoil the position of Centre of Pressure with i = 3°; join these two points by a straight line, and on this line mark a point P, 4/7 of its length from the chord of the lower Aerofoil; through this point P draw a line perpendicular to the aforementioned base line AB. This line we can take as representing accurately enough the line of Lift reaction on our *biplane*, for i = 3°. Through this same point P draw a line parallel to the Base line AB, which will represent the line of Dynamic Resistance of our biplane for 1 = 3°.

From the figures for our Aerofoil form, we shall measure off, to some suitable scale, a distance from P on the Lift re-action line to represent our biplane's K_y value i at = 3° and a distance from P on the Dynamic Resistance line to represent our biplane's K_x value at i = 3°. By drawing a parallelogram and its diagonal through our chosen point P, we now get a line (this diagonal), which represents the line of Total Re-action on our Biplane at i = 3°

Note that we take 4/7ths of the inter Aerofoil distance, not ½, for the top aerofoil does more work than the lower, in about the proportion of 4 to 3, at small values for i.

To same scale we must draw on another piece of tracing paper a side elevation of the Landing Gear.

We must now place these over our body drawing in guessed positions, keeping the base line AB on the Aerofoil drawing parallel to the axis of motor, and proceed to make a first calculation for position of CG. For this calculation we shall take horizontal Moments about the fore end of the body, and vertical Moments about the axis of the motor, as convenient datum lines, taking the weights of the various items multiplied by the normal distances of their CGs from these datum lines. We can fix pretty accurately the CGs of the items. I suggest taking the CG of the Aerofoils as slightly above the centre of a line joining the centre points of the lines which join the centre points of the spars of top and of bottom Aerofoils; slightly above (say 11/20ths above bottom), because the centre plane and its struts are at the top of the whole structure. The CG of the body alone may be taken as about 1/3 of its length from its fore end; the CG of the Tail unit as about 1 foot ahead of the rear end of the body; the CG of the Landing Gear, assuming a form as shown, as lying 12" ahead of, and 2" above, the wheel centres; the CG of a man sitting as about 12" ahead of the seat back and 12" above the seat bottom.

The CGs of the other items, tanks with petrol and oil, engine, engine mounting, engine cowling, seats, controls, instruments, Tail Skid, etc., are easy to fix accurate! v enough by inspection.

If our first shot for Aerofoil and Landing Gear position be out we must slide them to new positions, and try again, till we get the positions which answer our requirements.

We have now fixed up our outline design, and it remains to consider strength and stability, and then to finally check whether we have sufficient power for the high-speed and for the climb.

But before passing on let us note that the tank positions must be such that the CG alters little in horizontal position, whether they be full or empty, and they must also, of course, be of the required capacity. As it is almost impossible to keep the CG of both petrol and oil over the CG of the whole machine, and since for our motor the weight of petrol consumed per unit time is about six times the weight of oil consumed per unit time, we should keep the CG of the oil about six times as far (horizontally) from the total CG as is the CG of the petrol, and, of course, the tanks on opposite sides of the total CG.

Bearing this in mind, we get in the tanks as best we can.

Wing Strength.

For the strength of the wings, considered as an ordinary framed structure, we now have the overall sizes, the position of main aerofoil spars and of struts and ties. Considering each spar as a continuous beam and each aerofoil as uniformly loaded (its own weight being of course now *not* taken) for 5/6ths of its mean length, we must find the curve of bending moments and the reactions at the supports of each spar, firstly with the centre of pressure at its position nearest to the leading edge, and secondly at its position for full speed, which will be much further from the leading edge. The sections and materials of the spars must be chosen such that under neither of these conditions do the maximum calculated fibre stresses exceed 1/6th of the ultimate compressive strength of the material employed. This is the so-called "factor of safety" generally called for.

Similarly, the cross sections and material for each strut must be so chosen that (for a form of low head resistance), the maximum applied load does not exceed 1/6th of the ultimate strength, calculated by

Euler's formula for a pillar pin jointed at both ends.

Similarly, each stay cable should have an ultimate strength, taking into account any weakening due to splicing, etc., of at least 6 times the maximum pull we shall, from the before-mentioned calculations, find it subjected to.

I suggest considering the aerofoils as uniformly loaded for 5/6ths only of their total lengths, because, owing to end losses, the loading decreases towards the outer ends, and this assumption therefore gives a fairly accurate and a simple method of accounting for the actual distribution of loading over the aerofoil surfaces. Of course, the uniform loading used for the calculation must be adjusted so that total loading remains equal to the total weight for stress.

I shall not touch further on strength except to say that the same requirements hold throughout the machine, and the unfortunate designer is expected to be able to produce reasonable figures showing that his detail design is such that no part of the machine has a "factor of safety" of less than 6 under such condition, between slowest and fastest flying speeds, as imposes the greatest strain on such part.

STABILITY.

Now to consider stability and controllability, which resolves itself for us into determining the size of Tail Plane, Elevator, Fin, and Rudder and amount of dihedral angle of the Aerofoils for our design.

The full investigation of the stability of an aeroplane is necessarily an extremely long and difficult process, involving mathematics of a high order. I do not propose, however, to consider anything other than a few very simple methods in which by using data from model experiments and quite elementary mathematics we should arrive at decently satisfactory results. Thus, though they are all more or less interdependent, I propose to consider longitudinal or "pitching stability," lateral or "rolling stability," and directional or "yawing stability" separately.

Further, I shall take no account of the moment of inertia of the machine, though this has effects on the stability except to state that the moment of inertia about all three axes should be kept as low as possible, as much from strength as from stability considerations. A machine of large moment of inertia may perhaps be made as stable as one of small, but inasmuch it will rotate more slowly about any axis, it is highly probable that it will be subjected to greater local stress in a fluctuating wind, and it will answer more slowly to, and is therefore more likely to be locally stressed by, its controls.

First, then, for "longitudinal stability," and by this, I mean an innate tendency of the machine to preserve a constant attitude to its flight path—that is, to preserve a constant value of i for the aerofoils. For us this resolves itself into a determination of the size of the tail plane and elevators.

As you will have noted from our preceding curves for aerofoils, all along the range of i values useful for flight a curved aerofoil is unstable—that is, as i increases the CP moves forward, as i decreases the CP moves backwards; in both cases, therefore, the shift of CP tends to aggravate and not to stop the alteration of i value. Similarly, the body, which for low head resistance generally approaches a torpedo form, is instable for small angles to its flight path. It is left to the tail, therefore, to counteract the inherent instability of aerofoils and of body.

As for the form of calculation, this is best set out in tabular form (Fig. 12). In column 1 we have a values, a being the angle which the axis of the motor makes with the direction of flight; in column 2 the correspondong values for i, which in our case will be $a + 3°$ throughout; in column 3 corresponding values for KY, the lift coefficient of the aerofoils; in column 4 coeesponding values foe KX, the drift coefficient of the aerofoils; in column 5 values for total reaction coeffcient R,

which is, of course, $= \sqrt{K_Y{}^2 + K_X{}^2}$; in column 6 values for A × R, or aerofoil surface multiplied by total reaction coefficient ; column 7 is for L values, L being the perpendicular distance from CG of machine to line of action of R.

Column 8 is for A × R × L values, which is a function of the moment of the reaction on the aerofoils about the CG ; in column 9 we have values of β, or inclination of *tail plane* to line of flight, in our case β, $= a$ throughout ; in column 10 corresponding values of ky for *tail plane ;* and in column 11 corresponding values of kx for *tail plane ;* in column 12 values of total reaction coefficient r on tail plane, r being, of course, $= \sqrt{k_Y{}^2 + k_X{}^2}$; column 13 is for values of l, perpendicular distance from CG of machine to line of action of r ; column 14 for values of r × l ; column 15 is for values in column 9 divided by values in column 16—i.e., for $\dfrac{A \times R \times L}{l \times r}$—and

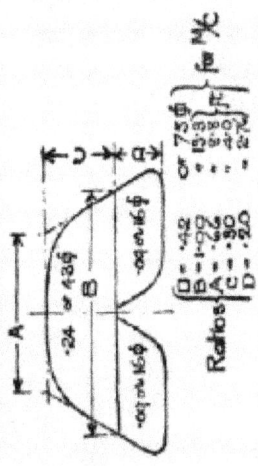

Fig 12.

PD = Ky for i'
PA = Kx " "
PD = R " "
CE = L " "

or QF = ky for θ'
QG = kx " "
QH = r " "
CK = L " "

CALCULATION FOR SIZE OF TAIL.

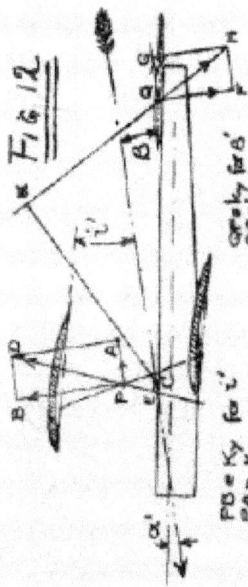

Ratios $\begin{cases} B = \cdot42 \\ B = 1\cdot00 \\ A = \cdot22 \\ D = \cdot20 \end{cases}$ or $\begin{cases} \cdot75\phi \\ 15\cdot3 \\ \cdot8\cdot8 \\ 4\cdot0 \\ \cdot27\phi \end{cases}$ for M/C

α°	i	Ky	Kx	$R=\sqrt{Ky^2+Kx^2}$	A×R (A=no·θ)	L	A×R×L	β	ky	kx	$r=\sqrt{ky^2+kx^2}$	L	tx×l	$\frac{A×R×L}{tx×L}$ for M/C
-5	-2	-·0007	-·00051	·00016	·0378	2·10	·0794	-5	-·00044	-·00011	·00045	13·7	·00646	12·9
-3	0	26	30	263	·1160	-70	·0812	-3	-·00027	-·00009	·00029	13·5	·00592	20·7
-1	+2	46	37	41	·2030	-20	·0406	-1	-·00009	-·00008	·00012	10·7	·00109	37·2
+1	4	64	45	64	·2820	+04	·0110	+1	·00009	·00006	·00012	10·7	·00109	10·1
3	6	83	63	932	·3660	·17	·062	3	27	9	29	13·5	·00392	15·8
5	8	102	89	1030	·4630	·30	·139	5	44	11	45	13·7	·00616	22·6
7	10	120	134	1206	·5300	·36	·191	7	61	15	62	13·6	·00843	22·7
9	12	136	163	1370	·6030	·42	·253	9	78	15	79	13·5	·01068	23·7
11	14	147	205	1485	·6330	·41	·268	11	94	18	96	13·3	·01274	21·0
13	16	150	250	1520	·6690	·40	·266	13	110	29	112	13·2	·01479	18·1

.....this gives us the required tail area necessary to just counteract the moment of reaction on the aerofoils, *assuming the tail as in undisturbed air.*

If we can get accurate model figures for the air reactions on the body of our machine, we should get out a second table, similar to the foregoing, to find the necessary area of the tail plane to counteract the instability of the *body*. But as we may not have these figures, and as the reaction on the body is comparatively small for a narrow form such as we are using, we may, in the absence of reliable model figures, neglect the second table, and merely add a small amount to the tail surface necessary for the aerofoils alone—say 1/10th.

As to how the figures for columns 7 and 13 are arrived at, in a similar manner to that in which we drew the line of total reaction on our biplane for i = 3°, we must draw a series of lines representing lines of total reaction on it for each of the i values in the table. We can then on our side elevation drawing measure the perpendicular distances from CG of machine to each of these lines, these distances being values for L, to scale of drawing. On the figure I have, for clearness, only drawn line for R at 1' value for i.

As for the tail plane, assuming we shall decide to employ one of the form shown, as a good compromise between strength and efficiency, if we have not figures for a model of this form it is probably accurate enough to take for it figures for a rectangular plane of aspect ratio 2 to 1.

As we do not know until after the calculation the size for our tail plane, we do not know exactly the position of its line of reaction. But the chord of the tail plane is fairly small compared to the distance from CG of machine to centre of pressure or tail plane, and smaller still is the *shift* of CP on tail plane compared to this distance. Hence we shall assume a point, say, 2 ins. above the top of the body and 2 ft. from the rear end of the body as the position of C of P on tail plane, and shall neglect the shift of CP. Of course, if on finishing the calculation we find that, for the tail plane size which we shall need, our guess is obviously a lot out, we must alter up and correct our table.

We shall take the required area of tail for our machine—that is to say, area of tail plane plus area of elevators—as twice the greatest area called for in the table. This seems rather a libel on our calculations, but the reason for this apparent large excess of tail area is that the tail is acting both in the down-draught from the aerofoils and—when the engine is running—in the slipstream of the propeller; both of these factors tend to *decrease the alteration of air flow relative to the tail*, when the attitude of the whole machine to its flight path is altered. That is to say, they both tend to decrease the correcting power of the tail.

This figure of half-value for the tail on the machine to Tail considered as in undisturbed air is approximately that found by recent experiments at the N.P.L.

Before leaving the question of longitudinal stability I would suggest that the value of total area of tail should be kept about as it would be found by the foregoing calculations for *any* machine, but the more the power of control required the greater should the relative area of elevators to tail plane be made. The ratio of elevator area to tail plane should lie between the limits of .6 to .4 and .3 to .7. Outside these limits we shall get a machine either heavy on the controls on the one hand, or slow to respond on the other. We shall use, therefore, a total area of 75 sq. ft., of which .43, or 32 sq. ft., is in the elevators, and we arrive at the sizes as shown.

Directional Stability.

Very briefly, for "directional" or "yawing stability," for us this now means size of rudder and fin required. I say rudder *and* fin for our machine, as I think it is safer to use a fin on large and heavy machines. On small and light machines, it is perhaps not necessary. Structurally, of course, the employment of a fin is of value.

We have at present few figures on which to base calculations for rudder size. The rudder and fin considered as a fixed surface must be large enough to counteract the inherent yawing instability of the body, also to counteract the yawing effect of the side surface of those parts of the landing gear which are ahead of the CG, and also to counteract the yawing effect of the propeller considered as a front fin.

We must also be sure that, when the rudder is set at about 5 degrees, say, it has ample power *additionally* to counteract the worst spinning moment induced by working the warp or ailerons. Unless we have model figures for yawing moments on the fuselage, and for drift on an aerofoil with ailerons at different attitudes, we had better determine our rudder area from figures for other machines as nearly like ours as possible which we know were satisfactory as regards their directional stability and control.

I suggest, then, using an empirical formula (Fig. 13):

$$C \, (s \times d) = S - \frac{S \times D}{2} + A$$

157

. . . in which s =area of rudder in sq. ft., d = distance of centre of area of rudder from CG of machine in feet, S is area of side elevation of body, aerofoils, landing-gear, and propeller in sq. ft., D = distance of centre of this area S *behind* CG, A is area of aerofoils in sq. ft. and C is a constant which we shall take as 1.7 from figures of other machines of this type.

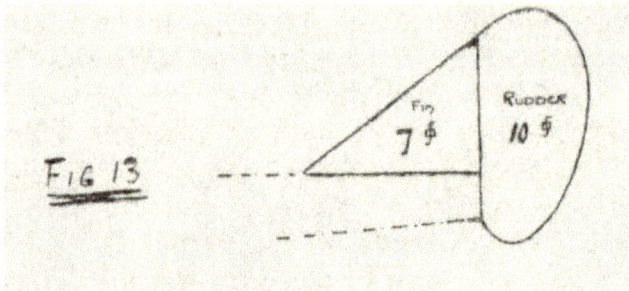

FIG 13

The value for body side area *in side elevation* of body, complete with all added top superstructure, cowling round motor, etc.

The value for side area of aerofoils is that of the aerofoils with their struts in side elevation, thus taking ccount of the fin area due to dihedral.

In our case, then, we have:

$$1.7 \times s \times 15 = 70 - \frac{70 \times 2.4}{2} + 440 \text{ or } s = 17$$

That is, we require a rudder + Fin area of 17 sq. ft. We shall dispose this in a form as shown in Fig. 13.

LATERAL STABILITY.

Let us consider the causes for possession of, or lack of, "lateral stability" in an aeroplane. An aeroplane is a body immersed in a fluid—air—and since its average density is very great compared to that of air, we consider it as supported only by the reaction of the air upon its lifting surfaces. That is to say, it is supported solely by reason of its speed relative to the air.

Now, for both of the stabilities we have already discussed—that is "pitching" stability and "yawing" stability—the flight path is approximately at right-angles to the axes of rotation. Hence a small rotation immediately induces a change of reaction upon the tail plane, or rudder, as the case may be, which tends to counteract the rotation. But when we come to consider the third form of stability— that is, "lateral" or "rolling" stability—we see that the rotation now takes place about an axis which is parallel, or very nearly parallel, to the flight path.

Hence rotation about the longitudinal axis, or rolling, will *by itself* produce no change whatever upon the air reactions on the machine; that is to say, if an aeroplane rotate about an axis parallel to its flight path, *no other motion being present,* no force is created to counteract the rotation.

However, when an aeroplane rolls, other movements do occur, and it is from these that we attain "lateral stability."

Let us consider, then (Fig. 14), an aeroplane flying steadily and horizontally and assume that some outside force, say a puff of wind, rolls it over slightly. We see that, as speed and therefore total reaction, RT, remain constant, and as the lift reaction is now out of line with the gravitational force, the vertical component of lift is now less than the gravitational force, and the horizontal component is unbalanced; that is to say, the machine will commence to drop and move sideways. Directly it commences to do this we *get* motion perpendicular to the axis of rotation and, if our surfaces are properly disposed, a righting moment therefrom.

Briefly, then, we see that, for "lateral stability," if the machine had a sideways velocity relative to the air, the resulting reactions on the whole machine must tend to raise the then leading aerofoil tip. This is the main reason why a dihedral angle for the aerofoils tends to give lateral stability. We also see that, if the outer shape of a machine remain the same, the higher the CG the greater the dihedral we shall need, and *vice versa.*

It is necessary for us, therefore, to calculate the vertical position of centre of projected side area of the whole machine less the aerofoils. I then suggest that, if this centre of area lie at the same height as the CG, give 3 *per cent,* dihedral angle to the aerofoils. If the centre of area lie *above* the CG, less dihedral should be given; if *below,* more dihedral should be given. For amount of increment (or decrement), I suggest 1° of dihedral per 15 value (in sq. feet x feet) of vertical moment of side area about CG. These figures are quite arbitrary ones and I cannot vouch for their suitability. They approximately represent current practice for machines of this type.

As you will note, in our design the centre of projected side area is considerably below the centre of gravity, .55 ft.; so, we had better decide to employ 5 *per cent,* dihedral angle.

We must note, before leaving the subject, that too much inherent

159

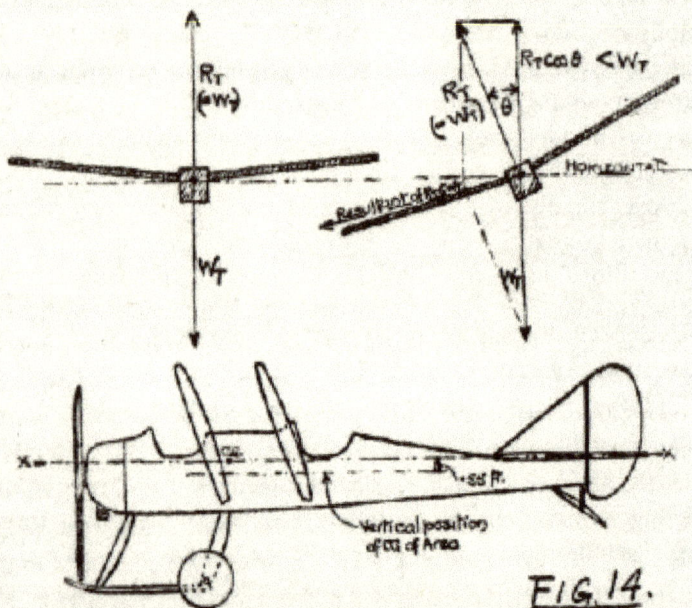

FIG. 14.

CALCULATION TABLE FOR VERTICAL C.G. OF AREA.

ITEM	A ($\square'$)	h (ft)	A × h.
Propeller	8·5	− ·9	− 2·2
Cowl	4·0	− ·5	− 2·0
Chassis Front Strut	1·0	−3·6	− 3·6
" Rear "	·8	−3·0	− 2·4
" Skid	1·0	−5·8	− 5·8
" Wheel	3·8	−4·9	− 18·6
Body below x−x	36·0	− ·9	− 32·4
" above "	8·6	+ ·5	+ 4·3
Aerofoil Struts	4·8	+1·2	+ 5·8
Fin	6·0	+1·0	+ 6·0
Rudder	9·0	+ ·9	+ 8·1
Tail Skid	·6	−1·8	− 1·1
TOTAL	78·1	·55	− 48·8

A = side elevation Area
of Item in $\square'$.

h = distance of Centre
of Area of Item above
or below Axis x−x

  + Above
  − below.

stability should not be given to an aeroplane. "Inherent stability," as I have used it, being a tendency of the machine to retain the same altitude to its flight path or to its *relative motion to the air*, it follows that the more stable is a machine in this sense the more does it tend to follow alterations in wind direction, and this quality in excess makes for discomfort in flying and danger in landing. Hence, we want to ensure that our machine has a *slight* margin of stability and that ample controlling power is afforded to the pilot to enable him to quickly alter at will its attitude in any direction.

PROPELLER THRUST.

We have now got our design temporarily completed; it remains to calculate the head resistance as accurately as possible and the propeller thrust, to see if we have sufficient power for the required high speed and climb and to check the balance of the machine.

Firstly, for the propeller thrust, I cannot attempt to touch propeller design in this paper; it is a subject for many papers in itself. I must merely refer to experimentally determined figures for propellers. We have a good many of these and can probably pick a form that will suit us. We will take it, then, that we have the curve of efficiency for a suitable propeller on a base of slip ratio at constant revolutions (Fig. 15).

The efficiency is expressed of course as:

$$\frac{\text{Useful work}}{\text{Total work}} \quad \text{or as} \quad \frac{\text{Thrust} \times \text{speed}}{\text{H.P given to propeller}}$$

$$\text{The slip ratio is } \frac{(p \times r) - V}{p \times r} \text{ where p is pitch of}$$

propeller in feet, r revs. per sec., and V is speed, i.e., speed of advance along axis in feet per sec.

Knowing the horse-power our motor gives at full normal revs., we can from this efficiency curve make another curve of our actual propeller thrust in lbs. on a base of speed of advance, *i.e.,* speed of aeroplane, in feet per sec.

HEAD RESISTANCE.

It remains to get figures for plotting a curve of total head resistance (in lbs.) of machine on this same base of speed in feet per sec.

For this we turn to the front elevation of our aeroplane (Fig. 16) and determine which parts lie within the propeller disc and which outside it. The parts which lie in the propeller disc, *i.e.,* in the slip-stream from the propeller, will be in a current of fairly constant speed *irrespective of* speed of machine.

161

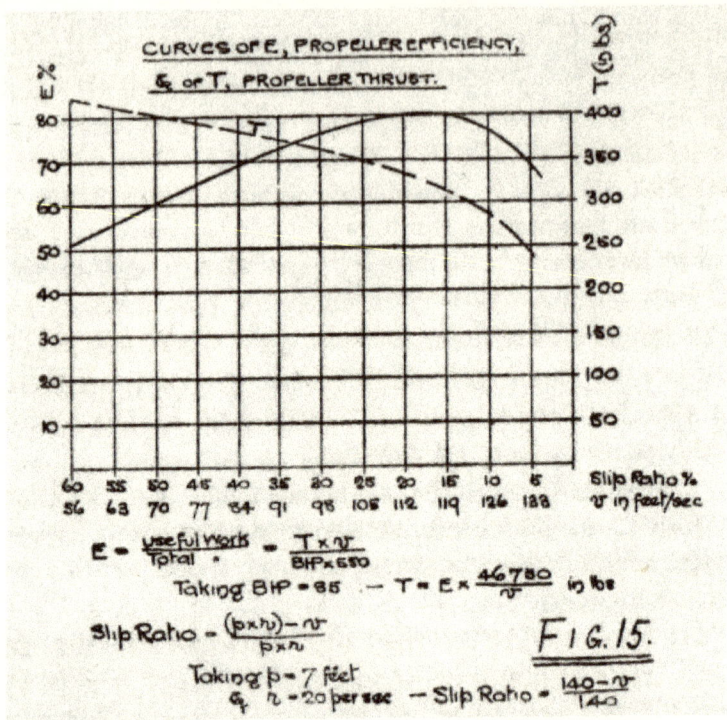

CURVES OF E, PROPELLER EFFICIENCY, & of T, PROPELLER THRUST.

Slip Ratio %	60	55	50	45	40	35	30	25	20	15	10	5
v in feet/sec	56	63	70	77	84	91	98	105	112	119	126	133

$$E = \frac{useful\ work}{Total} = \frac{T \times v}{BHP \times 550}$$

$$\text{Taking BHP} = 85 \quad - \quad T = E \times \frac{46750}{v} \text{ in lbs}$$

$$\text{Slip Ratio} = \frac{(p \times n) - v}{p \times n}$$

$$\text{Taking } p = 7 \text{ feet} \quad \& \quad n = 20 \text{ per sec} \quad - \quad \text{Slip Ratio} = \frac{140 - v}{140}$$

FIG. 15.

We make our calculation, therefore, in the form of two tables. The first table is for parts *in* the slip-stream, the second for parts *outside* it. In neither of these tables shall we include aerofoils, as the *total* reaction on these has already been dealt with in first balancing.

The coefficients for resistance for the different parts of our machine we must obtain from figures from model experiments, and of these we have a fair armament.

In both tables we find the resistance in lbs. for each item at some chosen fixed value of v; at the same time, we take, as you see, the moment of resistance of each item about the axis of the motor, vertically, of course, in order to obtain a figure for vertical position of centre of head resistance.

We must determine the vertical position of Centre of head resistance, less aerofoils of course, to see if there will be a thrust—head-resistance couple. If we find that there is one—that is to say, if the line of residual resistance is above or below the line of thrust—we must either (if practicable) alter the line of thrust or, by slightly altering the fore and aft position of the aerofoils, introduce an equal and opposite lift-weight couple to counteract the thrust-head resistance one.

162

TABLE 1. In Slip Stream

ITEM	A¢	Kx	R	h	R×h
Body	6.0	.0005	46.0	+.2	+9.2
Chassis Struts	1.80	.0002	4.0	-2.6	-10.4
" Cross bracing	.25	.0012	4.6	-2.6	-12.0
½ Axle	.15	.0002	1.4	-3.9	-5.5
Tail Skid	.40	.0004	2.5	-1.8	-3.2
Rudder	.40	.00008	.5	+2.4	+1.2
½ Tail & Stays	2.50	.00006	3.1	+1.0	+3.1
¼ C Plane Struts	.90	.0002	2.8	+3.0	+8.4
¾ " Bracing	.15	.0012	2.8	+3.0	+8.4
R₁ (TOTAL)	12.35	.00046	67.7	+.01	-.8

$U = 124$ fps $(130 - 5\%)$
$U^2 = 15400$

$R_1 = K_x \times A \times U^2$ lbs.
or $R_1 = 15400 K_x \cdot A$

FIG 16

TABLE 2. Outside Slip Stream.

ITEM	A¢	Kx	R	h	R×h
¼ Centre Plane Struts	.30	.0002	.6	+4.6	+2.8
¼ " Bracing	.05	.0012	.6	+4.6	+2.8
½ Tail Plane	2.40	.00008	1.9	+1.0	+1.9
Aerofoil Cables	2.70	.0012	32.0	+2.4	+76.8
" Struts	4.00	.0002	8.0	+2.5	+20.0
½ Axle	.45	.0002	.9	-3.9	-3.5
Wheels & Shock absorbers	1.00	.00045	4.5	-3.9	-17.6
Skids	.30	.0006	1.8	-4.0	-7.2
R₂ (TOTAL)	11.20	.00045	50.3	+1.51	+76.0

$U = 100$ fps
$U^2 = 10000$

$R_2 = K_x \times A \times U^2$
or
$R_2 = .00508 U^2$

At full speed i.e. 120 fps :-

$R_1 = 67.7$ lbs @ .01 ft below line of Thrust

$R_2 = .00508 \times 120^2 = 72.5$ lbs @ 1.51 ft above line of Thrust.

Hence total Residual Resistance @ 120 fps

= 140.2 lbs @ .77 feet above line of Thrust.

When $i = 2°$, $U = 98.8$ fps

Hence $R_2 = 39.5$ lbs & Total Residual Resistance = 107.2 lbs
@ .86 ft above line of Thrust.

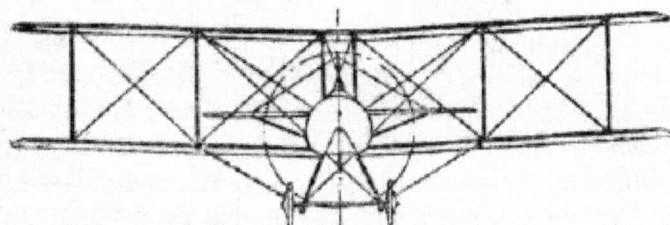

In the first of these tables, then, we shall take V as slightly below (say 5 *per cent*, below) the pitch speed of the propeller, and we shall take the total resistance R_1 of the items in this table as of the amount thereby found, and as constant for all speeds of the machine.

For our case we get R_1 as 67.7 lbs. acting .01 foot below line of thrust *and as constant*.

In the second table we shall take V as 100 f.p.s., being a convenient figure to work with, and the total resistance R_2 obtained is, of course, the resistance of all parts, except aerofoils, *outside* the slipstream at 100 f.p.s. We take R_2 as *varying* as V^2.

In our case, therefore, we get a second table resistance R_2 of 50.3 lbs. at 100 feet per sec.—that is to say, R_2 = .00503 v^2 lbs. and acts 1.51 ft. *above* line of thrust. We see then that for the design as so far got out the line of total residual resistance is going to be considerably above the line of thrust. At maximum speed required, 120 f.p.s., it is going to be 140.2 lbs. acting .77 foot *above* the line of thrust. So, we must either raise the line of thrust or shift the aerofoils aft slightly. We should, however, make the necessary correction for balance, for that speed at which i for aerofoils = 3°, as then the tail is floating.

Now when i = 3°, Ky = .00055, hence v must be 88.5 feet per sec., thence R_2, = 39.5 lbs., and thence *total residual resistance* R_2 + R_2 = 107.2 lbs. and acts at .55 ft. above line of thrust. We shall therefore decide to shift our line of thrust up .6 foot, which will give a satisfactory balance and will have the additional advantages of bringing the line of thrust nearer to the CG and of slightly cutting down landing gear height, and therefore weight and head resistance.

We *should* now correct our tables for CG and for residual head resistance; this would be a repetition of the previously described calculations, and the figures for amount of total residual head resistance which we have already obtained would hardly be altered, certainly not *increased*, by this raising of line of thrust. Hence, as we can use them as they are for looking into the remaining points, I omit, for the sake of brevity, correcting up these tables here.

Finally, then, we turn again to our model aerofoil figures to obtain the remaining part of the total head resistance, the "drift" of our aerofoils (Fig. 17). From the Ky values we first determine the speeds corresponding to several different values for i, say for i = 1°, 4°, 7°, 10°, 13°, 16°.

Taking into account the variation of lift to drift with log AV before quoted, we find then the drift (RD) of our machine's aerofoils at these different values for v.

By our previously determined equation we find the values for part R_2 of residual resistance at these speeds; whilst part R_1 of residual resistance is constant and already obtained. So now we can plot out our curve of total resistance, or $R_1 + R_2$, + RD.

If from these curves of propeller thrust and of total resistance now obtained, we see that the resistance be less than, or equal to, the thrust at the maximum speed we are asked to accomplish, then this speed is, presumably, attainable.

TABLE FOR RESISTANCES

i	v (fps)	R_1 (lbs)	R_2 (lbs) $=.0053\,v^2$	L/D Model	L/D Full	RD (lbs) $=\frac{800\times D}{v}$	R_T (lbs) $=R+R_1+R_2$
1	120	68	72	10.0	11.7	162	302
4	89	"	40	16.2	21.6	88	196
7	74	"	28	12.4	13.9	137	233
10	65	"	21.	9.6	10.4	182	271
13	60	"	18	7.7	8.2	232	318
16	58	"	17	6.0	6.4	297	382

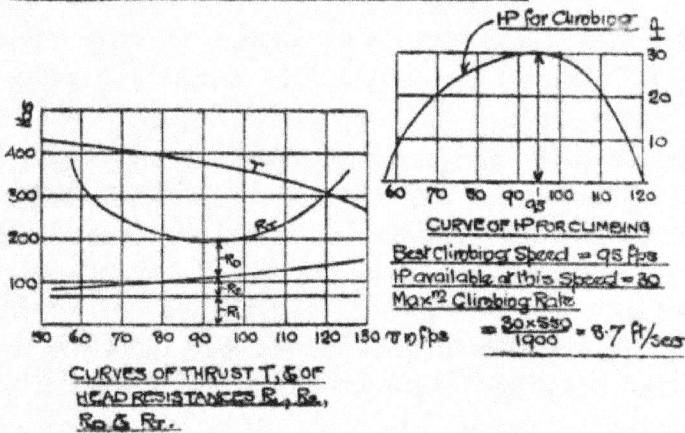

FIG. 17

CURVE OF HP FOR CLIMBING

Best Climbing Speed = 95 fps
HP available at this Speed = 30
Max^m Climbing Rate $= \frac{30\times550}{1900} = 8.7$ ft/sec

CURVES OF THRUST T, & OF HEAD RESISTANCES R_1, R_2, R_D & R_T.

CLIMBING SPEED.

It remains to find the greatest possible climbing speed and see if the final requirement can be fulfilled.

The vertical height of the thrust curve above the total resistance curve at any point along the base gives us the surplus thrust at the corresponding base line value for speed.

This surplus thrust multiplied by value for speed, gives us a value for foot lbs. per sec. available for climbing.

This value we may plot as a final curve of power available for climbing.

We then take the maximum Value given us by the highest point on our curve), noting the speed at which this optimum value is attained.

Then our optimum value of power for climbing ÷ the total weight of machine gives us best climbing rate in feet per sec.

If this be decently over the requirement, we can consider the preliminary design as finished.

In Conclusion.

In the first over-all design, methods for arriving at which I have attempted to outline, no pains should be spared to get the best and most compact disposition of external parts, and the best sizes and forms for them. In the structural design, which I have not touched upon, every detail should be considered most carefully to ensure that each is as simple and compact, and, therefore, as light for its strength as possible, and that for each is chosen the best material.

If this be done, using with due common sense every source of reliable data, and doing everything methodically and thoroughly, it is highly probable that the results will be good, and if one goes on working thus in subsequent designs, altering up empirical constants as found necessary or advisable from increasing experience, one will design better machines, and will know why they are improved.

It is because this system of methodical improvement is, I think, the basis of all true engineering advance, and because little thrashing out of tables and formulae has been done so far (or at any rate published) from the data presently available, that I have tried in this paper to outline some methods for doing so.

I am painfully aware that much necessary matter has perforce been left out, and that much of what I have said is incorrect, but if it prove of interest or instructive, if it help in any way the betterment of this branch of engineering science, I am amply repaid for what time and effort it has cost me.